The Self-Preservation GUIDE

HOW TO LEAVE A TOXIC RELATIONSHIP & CHANGE YOUR LIFE ...

KRISTINA RUTH

Author: Kristina Ruth

First Published: February 2021 by KR Publishing Pty Ltd, Level 1 CUA Plaza, 54-56 Baden Powell Street, Maroochydore, 4558.

© 2021 KR Publishing Pty Ltd ABN 90 645 430 477

All rights reserved.

This publication is copyright protected work. Other than for the purposes of and subject to the conditions prescribed under the *Copyright Act 1968* (Cth), no part of it may in any form, or by any means be reproduced in whole or in part, stored, posted on the Internet, or transmitted in any form or by any means whether electronically, mechanically, by photocopying, recording, or any other means, without permission from the Publisher.

Although the author and publisher have made every effort to ensure that the information in this book was correct at press time, the author and publisher do not assume and hereby disclaim any liability to any party for any loss, damage, or disruption caused by errors or omissions, whether such errors or omissions result from negligence, accident, or any other cause.

This book is not intended as a substitute for medical, health, well-being, or financial advice. The reader should do their due diligence or consult the relevant expert agencies or organisations listed at the back of this book or one of the reader's own choosing.

The publisher and the author are providing this book and its contents on an "as is" basis and make no representations or warranties of any kind with respect to this book or its contents. The publisher and the author disclaim all such representations and warranties, including but not limited to warranties of healthcare for a particular purpose.

The content of this book is for informational purposes only and is not intended to diagnose, treat, cure, or prevent any condition or situation. You understand that this book is not intended as a substitute for consultation with a licensed practitioner. Please consult with your own physician, healthcare, or legal specialist regarding the suggestion and recommendations made in this book. The use of this book implies your acceptance of this disclaimer.

The publisher and the author make no guarantees concerning the level of success you may experience by following the advice and strategies contained in this book, and you accept the risk that results will differ for each individual.

The author has tried to recreate events, locales, and conversations from her memories of them. In order to maintain their anonymity in some instances the author has changed some identifying characteristics and details to protect the privacy of individuals.

The moral rights of the author have been asserted.

All inquiries are to be addressed to the publisher.

Facebook: The Self Preservation Guide

Production by: Bermingham Books.

Printed and bound in Australia by: Ingram Spark.

ISBN: 978-0-6450525-5-8

The symbolism of the tree on the cover is significant to me.

The tree will weather a lot throughout it's lifetime; drought, floods, fires and changing seasons. However, its roots remain firm, keeping the tree alive.

The tree represents you. You will endure many seasons of good and bad times throughout your life. It's unavoidable. However, always remember that the roots of your tree, representing your soul, will be what provides you the strength to endure whatever life throws at you. Nothing or no one can ever take that away from you.

DEDICATION

I dedicate this book to you.
For helping yourself
or someone else,
take the first step in
changing your life.

CONTENTS

Foreword 1

Introduction 4

UNDERSTANDING WHAT TOXIC RELATIONSHIPS LOOK LIKE

Chapter 1 - For better or for worse 10

Chapter 2 - What does abuse look like?............................... 21

Chapter 3 - How safe is your relationship?
A relationship health check 36

Chapter 4 - The warning signs.. 48

Chapter 5 - Use your intuition, good vibrations 59

Chapter 6 - Judgement 66

Chapter 7 - Addicted to love 74

Chapter 8 - What if you decide to stay? 80

Chapter 9 - Power and control... 86

BREAKING FREE OF TOXIC RELATIONSHIPS

Chapter 10 - Preparing for freedom 101

Chapter 11 - Keeping yourself safe 110

Chapter 12 - Your support network 120

HEALING AND LIFE AFTER A TOXIC RELATIONSHIP

Chapter 13 - Healing 127

Chapter 14 - Core Values 133

Chapter 15 - Building your new life 145

Chapter 16 - Time to thrive 155

Afterword 165

Thank you 169

Further reading 170

Resources 171

Bibliography 181

Biography 185

Contact us 186

FOREWORD

This clever, well-written, and thought-out book is a valuable resource for anyone who wants to leave the clutches of a toxic relationship and build a brand new, safe, and happy life for themselves. Navigating the challenging world of separation and divorce is tricky at best, and there are many things you don't think about while in the emotional prelude to it. Preparing effectively is the key to steering yourself successfully through these muddy waters, and Kristina's book helps you to do just that.

I wish someone had told me all the essential things I needed to think about, action and have prepared, before I went through my separation. It can be completely overwhelming for the unprepared, particularly if you have safety concerns or have children. Kristina's book will help not only help you save your sanity, but a small fortune in time, money, and emotional overload.

This book has been Kristina's passion for many years and to see it published is truly remarkable, and testament to her commitment to helping others. She has pooled her vast, well-researched knowledge and insight, powerfully guiding those going through separation and divorce with succinct tools, strategies, and resources in this 'quick, easy-to-read' guide.

Along with practical steps, Kristina also identifies toxic red flags and relationship characteristics to watch out for—at home, at work or in our personal lives, and shows you how to break free from those relationships to be free, happy, and safe to regain your confidence, rebuild your life, and truly thrive.

This book will be life changing for so many. It offers solutions to your challenges, expert advice in all areas from amicable separation to fleeing abusive relationships safely and rebuilding a new life solo.

As a Senior Financial Adviser specialising in advocating women's rights, who often sees women in the aftermath of their separation, I will be gifting this book to all clients I work with who are embarking on the separation and divorce journey, as I know it will be instrumental in providing them with the first step towards their very bright future.

Jodie Nolan
MBA (Applied Finance)
Senior Financial Adviser & Economist

INTRODUCTION

Preparing to flee a toxic relationship or domestic violence takes time, thought, strategy, courage, and effort. I have encountered many women, over the years, who wanted to leave their abusive relationships, but who felt trapped by the virulent grip of domestic violence.

I've written this book for them, the ones who survived and the ones who will, and as a commemoration of those who didn't get out, but who lost their lives to domestic abuse.

I have spoken to many women who escaped and to the experts, who help women rebuild themselves and leave toxic relationships behind.

This book is intentionally short, easy-to-read and to the point. That's because I understand that when you're living in a toxic, controlling, or abusive environment, you don't have time to digest large in-depth content. Therefore, I've kept it short and sweet, so you can pick it up, quickly go to the phase you are in, and read the steps you can take to move forward.

The following pages are full of practical information, help, resources and encouragement to help anyone—man or woman—break free from an abusive relationship, be it in the home, at work or in their personal life.

As you read through The Self-Preservation Guide, you will be able to examine your current relationships and decide if you have any of the warning signs of toxic people in your life.

It is important to know yourself and to understand the negative impact others have on you. Having all the information means you are able to decide if these toxic people need to be removed from your life. This is called self-preservation.

Even though some people find it uncomfortable to talk about this topic, the reality is that a high percentage of people are living in abusive relationships, right now. Add to that the ones working in an abusive workplace, or that have other abusive relationships in their life, and you'll quickly realize that it's definitely not something that is all that far removed from your own world. Even if you aren't experiencing it, someone close to you will be and this book will help you to help them.

You don't need to make the break, only after you're broken to the core and have no options left. That's why this book is so important; it will show you the warning signs and allow you to make a move, before you end up in a dangerous situation that is out of your control. This book will show those, who are suffering every day and not thriving, and who need to break free in order to find real happiness and self-love—there ARE ways.

If you feel as if you can't reach out to anyone and be honest about your situation, this book is for you. If you feel you can reach out to someone, but you don't know where to begin, this book is for you. If you don't know whether you are in a toxic situation, but can't understand why you're not happy, this book is for you. If you're desperately looking for a way to regain your confidence, your self-esteem, and your strength, this book is for you.

No one is immune to domestic violence—it does not discriminate. It affects people of all races, religions, and status. There are far too many people out there in situations that make them feel unsafe, compromised, used, and battered, and who have ultimately realised that their confidence has been eroded; this book is for you, too.

Enabling the behaviour of others and weathering emotional abuse takes its toll. Riding the emotional psychological rollercoaster, to keep your family together with compassion and kindness, can be fatiguing.

Take a look at your life. Do you cry yourself to sleep? Do you feel so desperately trapped in the grip of domestic violence that you can't breathe? Do you feel as if you are suffocating in the toxicity of another person?

Does holding the vision and illusion of the perfect life drain you of all your energy? Do you feel as though your soul has disappeared? Are you not facing the truth and disappearing into your 'bubble' of a false sense of reality? Are you living a nightmare, consumed by fear, emptiness, despair, and unhappiness?

Do you want to change your life? Do you want to leave your toxic relationship and be happy again? Do you feel trapped and wish your life were different? Eventually, something will have to give.

Where do you begin?

One step at a time…

Right now, you can change your whole world, armed with the information, strategies, resources, and know-how you have in your hands. After speaking to women who have done just that, I can say hand-on-heart, life as you know it can be far better than your wildest dreams.

You deserve a better life, and this will be the first step in what will inevitably become the bright and beautiful future you have wished for. I look forward to helping you step out of the life you don't want and to rebuild a life you do want.

Kristina

UNDERSTANDING WHAT TOXIC RELATIONSHIPS LOOK LIKE

CHAPTER 1
For better or for worse

One of the most important things to understand is that our belief systems either help or hinder us, and how this happens.

When we are born, we enter the world with a clean slate and no preconceived beliefs. Our personalities and belief systems are shaped by our early learning from the people who come into our lives—our parents, siblings, friends, teachers, neighbours and social groups.

Other people's beliefs and behaviours have a great impact on us. We take many of them on board, regardless of whether we have consciously explored if they are true or not, or whether we see it or not.

The greater percentage of our core beliefs are passed onto us. We inherit them and they take up residence in our psyche, like uninvited guests. The important thing to realise is that these beliefs govern many of the choices we make, yet most are not our own. Belief systems dominate our social fibre and culture.

You have to wonder why we don't give more consideration to something that has such a massive impact on how we go about our day.

Until you have explored your own set of beliefs, you really have no true idea of whether they work for your betterment or your detriment.

So this is your starting point; your road back to who you really are, and what you really want—the happiness and confidence to live the life you truly deserve without fear.

Our culture has trained us to believe the long-written vows we recite when we marry, such as 'for better or for worse'. Of course, everyone aspires to be there for their partner in the good days and the bad, but how much bad is bearable? How much bad is healthy? How much bad do you need to weather, before it strips you of all the good things about yourself?

The 'worse' part of 'better or worse', pretty much sums up the generation that put up with the bad behaviour, no matter how poorly they were treated, because marriage was for life and that's what they had signed up for. The generation before us, really believed that, although it was almost unbearable to live with their spouse's behaviour, they had vowed to love them for better or for worse anyway.

Our own beliefs can be powerful and when we look at how and why we end up in unsafe relationships and toxic situations, the reason usually centres on our belief system.

Our society and women, in particular, have tended to sacrifice their own happiness for the sake of their partners. This is a belief system that was inherited from generations of this behaviour. Now, however, it's time to change the way we look at relationships and our belief systems.

Self-realisation and self-awareness are essential to understanding yourself and realising where your weaknesses lie. We are emotional beings and sometimes our emotions get the better of us. It's about separating the emotion from the facts, and that can be a lot harder to do than it sounds, because our emotions are wrapped up in every decision we make in life.

We put up with situations and enable others' bad behaviours, because we let emotions become a weakness, which can, ultimately, lead to other people's taking advantage of us while we are in that emotional state.

We learn to put up with bad behaviour and make excuses for it, 'Oh, it's been a bad day', 'It's been stressful lately, etc. We allow ourselves to accept fewer than our fundamental needs, as we want to keep the peace and make things better by sweeping it all under the carpet.

Initially, we turn a blind eye, believing there is nothing wrong with them, and we make excuses for them, such as they had a tough upbringing. In the end, self-sacrifice dominates, and we find ourselves consistently compromising ... we walk on eggshells, to prevent the other person from causing an embarrassing or humiliating scene! They manipulate us into believing we are in the wrong—all the time. They never apologise or take any responsibility. It is always our fault.

Eventually they may begin manipulating us into doubting ourselves—our memory, our judgement, and even our own sanity. This is called gaslighting. Gaslighting is a classic tactic that abusers use, intentionally, to twist our perception of reality for their own gain and it's rampant in toxic relationships.

Even if you have never been emotionally abused, personally, you'll have seen gaslighting in action, behind these common statements:

- You're overreacting
- You need help
- I didn't do that
- You're upset over nothing

- You must be confused again
- Just calm down
- You're so dramatic
- I never said that
- Why are you so defensive?
- What are you talking about?
- It's your fault
- You're so sensitive
- You twist things
- Stop imagining things
- I was just joking
- You're remembering things wrong
- There's always something with you

If you no longer feel like the person you used to be, or feel more anxious and less confident than you used to, then you might have been gaslighted. Do you wonder if you're being too sensitive? Or do you feel as if everything you do is wrong? Do you always take the blame and feel as if it's always your fault when things go wrong?

The big one is … do you apologise all the time? Or do you sense that something's wrong, but you can't identify what it is? Do you question whether your response to your partner is appropriate? Lastly, do you make excuses for your partner's behaviour?

Sound familiar? The cause of their problem is always deflected onto you. They can't and won't take any responsibility for their actions—there's no point even expending the energy. They make you feel as if you're doing everything wrong, and after a while you feel as if you're going crazy; that's all part of their control. Once they have control of you, they know how to keep you believing you are the problem, and every time you try to reason with them it escalates further, until you submit.

Unbelievably, even in today's culture in Australia, the statistics for domestic violence are staggering.

One in three women will experience violence from a current or former partner. Even more horrifically, more than one woman is killed by her current or former partner every week, in domestic violence-related situations.

In 1996, only 19% of women, who experienced physical assault by a male perpetrator, reported it to the police. This number rose to 36% in 2005, but it is still significantly lower than it should be.

According to White Ribbon, a not-for-profit organisation for the prevention of domestic violence, one in four women has experienced emotional abuse, by a current or former partner, since the age of fifteen. These numbers are increasing every single year.

- One in five women has experienced sexual violence, since the age of 15
- 85% of Australian women have been sexually harassed
- Almost 40% of women continue to experience violence from their partner, while temporarily separated
- One in six women has experienced stalking, since the age of 15
- Intimate partner violence is a leading contributor to illness, disability and premature death in women aged 18-44

- One in six girls had experienced abuse before the age of 15
- The children of mothers, experiencing domestic violence, have higher rates of social and emotional problems than other children
- One in three women, aged 18-24, has experienced sexual harassment
- One in three young people don't think that controlling someone is a form of violence.

Another massive contributor to toxic relationships is narcissistic personality disorder. This is a disorder where a person has an inflated sense of their self-importance. Some signs to look out for are an excessive need for admiration, a disregard for other's feelings, and an inability to handle any criticism. The biggest sign, however, is a sense of entitlement!

That being said, it is really easy not to notice the signs, until you are well into the relationship. Narcissists are usually charming at first, and the relationship starts off like a fairy tale. They constantly 'love bomb' you with text messages and tell you over and over again how much they love you. They will constantly talk about themselves and their achievements, and this confidence and self-esteem can be very attractive, in the beginning!

However, although they feed you constant compliments and praise you, they lack empathy, and will be unable to feel how you might be feeling. Ultimately, narcissism is selfish behaviour. It creates a toxic relationship, because your partner is egotistic at your expense and is unable to consider your feelings at all.

It can be confronting to realise that you are in a toxic relationship, and even more so when you understand how these behaviours and beliefs have been instrumental in bringing you to where you are, now. Facing yourself is not easy, nor is realising that what you believe about yourself has ultimately led you along your journey—but they have. Your beliefs and your partner's behaviour have also moulded you into the person you are.

The negative impact that another person can have on you is astonishing! Their toxic energy and beliefs can make you feel as if you are the one going crazy. They can make you feel as if you are seriously losing your mind, until eventually you give in to their negative power over you like a wave washing over you in the ocean. You start to constantly give in to the negativity, until it begins to feel as if you are drowning and can't breathe!

CHAPTER 2
What does abuse look like?

When you begin asking yourself the question, 'How did I end up here?', then the bubble that you've been living in is about to burst wide open.

I have spoken with many women, and that's how I know that the first—difficult—step is recognising there is a problem. One of the women I spoke with (let's call her Jane) said to me, 'I lived in my bubble for years, naive and refusing to see the truth'.

Domestic and family violence and abusive relationships take many different forms. Don't be fooled into believing that domestic or social abuse is only physical, or that it's the only kind of abuse that can land you in an emergency ward. Actions or words that hurt, demoralise, intimidate, manipulate, suppress you into a form of submission or make you afraid, are all forms of domestic violence.

As strong as you may be, naturally, emotional and psychological abuse can be just as dangerous and life threatening as physical violence. For years, Jane didn't think that her situation was 'domestic violence', because she wasn't being physically hit or punched. Even though she was pushed and shoved, she made excuses for it, took the blame, and apologised, just to diffuse the argument.

When you're living in your own bubble, you may think the statistics don't apply to you. You might tell yourself that your situation 'isn't that bad'. Usually, abuse starts off as small incidents, such as a cutting remark, a verbal backlash, or a little shove, and escalates from there. Most women who have lived, or are living, with domestic violence, don't even know that they are!

Tragically, at its peak, abuse can result in death and, although these deaths are occasionally reported in the media, too often they go unseen.

Even the healthiest of relationships will experience a disagreement or two. Some counsellors even say that it's healthy to debate with your partner, from time to time. However, the difference is that in an abusive situation opinions, ideas, concerns or issues are not raised in a respectful way, and are often expressed in a heated manner with yelling and aggression.

Domestic violence can occur within:

- Intimate personal relationships (including same-sex relationships)
- Spousal relationships (married, de facto, registered, ex-partners, parents of the abuser or the defendant)
- Engagement relationships (two people who are or were engaged to be married)
- Couple relationships (two people in a relationship)
- Family relationship (two people, one of whom is a relative by blood or marriage of the other person in the relationship). At one time, this referred predominately to the parental relationship within a family, but now more cases being reported where the abuser and the victim are other family members, including siblings.
- Care relationship (one person in the relationship is dependent on the other for their day-to-day activities). This can also extend to relationships you have in social, work and learning environments of course.

What we need to remember is this; any person, who uses abusive and/or violent behaviour to gain power and control over another, by instilling fear in them, is an abuser.

Any person who feels fearful and intimidated by threats or actual violence is a victim of abuse.

A large number of cases of abuse and violence don't begin, or escalate, until the relationship is well established; e.g., after couples move in together, become engaged, get married or—very commonly—when the woman falls pregnant.

Reading through the following might be really difficult for you. However, in order to escape your situation, you will need to remove the blame from yourself, as well as the guilt, the fear, and the shame. Remember that abusers use your fear to gain power and control within a relationship and to manipulate you.

Domestic and family violence can occur in many forms and isn't confined to any one community, social class, and age, or cultural or geographic demographic. There are many forms of domestic and family violence. Some will be obvious, some won't be. They include:

Physical abuse

Physical violence is the act of using physical force to invoke fear, or cause pain or harm to someone else and it includes:

- Pushing or shoving
- Hitting or slapping
- Kicking or punching
- Choking or strangling
- Throwing or breaking things
- Using weapons
- Physical restraint
- Threatening to, or actually, harming people, pets, or those close to you in order to frighten, intimidate, and force you into submission
- Physically restricting a person's ability to move, such as locking someone in a room or a house, or tying them up.

Emotional and verbal abuse

This is unseen abuse and is not always easy to identify. Although it doesn't inflict physical injury, it can be just as dangerous and life-threatening as physical abuse. An emotionally abusive partner can cause incredible damage to a person's mental health, by eroding their feelings of self-worth and confidence. In some cases this behaviour leaves the abused person completely unable to function, and they become reliant on the very person who is inflicting the abuse.

Abusers do this through:

- Yelling at, swearing at, or insulting
- Bullying, putting down, criticising or belittling
- Public embarrassment and name calling
- Intimidation or threats intended to create fear
- Isolating the abused person from friends, family, and their safety net
- Aggressive conduct when in social or family groups, to alienate the abused person

- Ignoring the presence or conversation of the abused person to create feelings of rejection and lowered value
- Threatening to commit suicide or self-harm to intimidate and control
- Threatening to 'out' the abused person to others, or to divulge personal information that they have kept private for personal or safety reasons

Sexual abuse

Being abused wears away and strips you of your personal power. Generally, sexual abuse happens between two people who know each other or who are in a relationship. It is the act of forcing demeaning sexual activity on another person without their consent. Often it is combined with physical and emotional abuse. It affects a person's physical, emotional, and mental health and—in many cases—results in anxiety and post-traumatic stress disorder.

Sexual abuse includes:

- Penetration, rape, and rape with an object

- Non-consensual force, deliberate causing of pain during sex, or forcing someone to perform sexual acts
- Coercing or forcing someone to have sex with another person or to take part in a sexually-oriented activity, including exposing them to porn, or forcing them to undress
- Making unwanted, crude, or degrading sexual remarks or insults about a person's body or sexual performance
- Assaulting genitalia
- Uninvited touching
- Withholding of sex as a punishment, to control someone
- Using sex to coerce compliance

Economic abuse

You would be surprised at just how often this occurs. Many people think that the days of one person's controlling the financial incomings and outgoings of another is a thing of the past. However it's a common form of abuse and is often classed as the most subtle type. Its very nature, mind you, is far from subtle. It is no less damaging than other types of abuse. Do you feel as though you have to ask permission to spend your money? Do you feel as if your partner questions everything you purchase and that you always end up in an argument?

In economic abuse, the abuser:

- Controls the finances, in order to tear down the abused person's independence
- Limits spending, to isolate and take away the abused person's freedom and capacity to do anything outside the home
- Refuses to allow the abused person to seek or keep employment, so that they are tied to the abuser and completely dependent on them
- Claims the abused person's earnings

- Forbids access to accounts or money, without asking for permission, this even includes the abused person's own earnings, which are completely under the abuser's control
- Confiscates personal or essential items of significance or meaning
- Disposes of property, against the abused person's wishes, and without a lawful excuse
- Coerces or deceives the abused person into signing documents for control or financial gain
- Withdrawal of financial support

Social abuse

This form of abuse is generally the first stage of control, and precedes an escalation in the types of abuse. It can go on for long periods of time before being noticed. It's subtle, deceptive, and invasive and is used to manipulate, coerce, control, and, sometimes, completely isolate a person from their social network.

Social abuse includes:

- Monitoring and controlling where, when and for how long a person goes anywhere
- Restricting or preventing the abused person from contacting their family or friends
- Monitoring the abused person's phones, computers, or other devices without their permission
- Constantly criticising the abused person's friends or family
- Purposely removing access to communication avenues
- Following the abused person or stalking them by foot, car, or device; constantly contacting them by phone, text message, and emails, or waiting and watching outside their home or work

Technological abuse

In today's digital age, this type of abuse is rife, but it's no less acceptable. This type of abuse has already contributed to a staggering number—hundreds of thousands—who commit suicide every year.

Technological abuse includes:

- Hacking into the abused person's personal emails or social network accounts (e.g. Facebook)
- Posting online abusive statements, containing explicit and implicit threats, or images of the abused person without their consent
- Installing GPS tracking devices, spyware, and hidden recording devices without the abused person's knowledge

Spiritual abuse

This refers to the denial or misrepresentation of someone's spiritual beliefs, or the abuser's forcing their beliefs and practices onto someone else.

Spiritual abuse includes:

- Forcing someone to attend religious activities
- Preventing a person from taking part in their religious or cultural practices
- Manipulating spiritual or religious beliefs and practices to warrant abuse and violence

- Exploiting their beliefs to gain control
- Ridiculing someone's beliefs

Note: Many of the above descriptions, such as for sexual abuse, physical violence and stalking, are criminal offences in Australia. Victims should call the police on 000.

As you can see domestic abuse and violence take many different forms, but there is one common thread and that is control. Having control over another person, by inflicting fear, submission, and/or shame, gives an abuser power. As a victim, this is terrifying and robs you of your sense of self-worth and security.

Even if your partner, or ex-partner, is apologetic and loving after an attack, it's STILL abuse. It still has the potential to become much more lethal as time goes on. The same is true when there has been 'only one or two' incidents of abuse. Studies have shown that in these less frequent cases, incidents have still continued. Rather than being one-off occurrences, they will worsen. It's important to watch out for the red flags that put you or your family in harm's way, or which compromise your well-being physically, emotionally, socially, economically, or spiritually.

You must be honest, if you want to leave a toxic person and become a survivor. You must let go of the shame and the stigma concerning domestic violence. It's dangerous to stay in your bubble and pretend you don't see the signs. It's also soul-destroying and, even in moments where you can say you are happy under the circumstances, deep down you know that it will be short-lived. You know what isn't normal. Eventually you may even be setting your kids up for relationship failures, and depriving them of the chance to experience true happiness and safety.

CHAPTER 3

How safe is your relationship?
A relationship health check

How safe is your relationship? How safe are you? Is your relationship healthy?

Let's take a closer look and find out what is healthy and what is toxic?

The most obvious sign of being in a toxic or abusive relationship is feeling fearful of the other person. Deep down in your gut you know when something's not right. When you are afraid of someone in your life, it's a clear sign that abuse is at work. It's a powerful red flag, which we shouldn't ignore—but we do.

Why?

Dealing with unbearable fear can render you physically inactive. In that moment, it's almost impossible to think straight, let alone act, run, escape, or avoid the threat you're facing.

Paralysing fear is truly terrifying. It's triggered by an adrenaline rush that's caused by instinctive animal behaviour. We've all experienced the fight or flight rush that overtakes our bodies, when we are faced with an unbearable life-threatening fear.

Anxiety attacks your body until you are paralysed by fear, or literally, scared stiff and you break out in a cold sweat. Your breathing is so shallow you feel as if you're not breathing at all and you can't get air into your lungs.

Your anxiety goes through the roof as your nervous system reacts to the threat. It's a vicious circle; as each time you become aware of what's about to happen, the fear heightens.

If your partner does any of the following, it is a clear sign that you are in an unhealthy relationship. Do they:

- Show signs of extreme jealousy and possessiveness
- Not let you have friends, or constantly check up on you
- Try to control you by being bossy, give you orders, make all the decisions and not listen to your opinions at all
- Put you down and tell you that you would be nothing without them
- Threaten or intimidate you
- Have a history of violence
- Get too serious about the relationship too fast
- Abuse alcohol or other drugs and pressure you to take them

- Have a history of failed relationships and blame the other person for all the problems
- Make your friends and family uneasy or concerned for your safety
- Try to harm you physically, or to force you to do something sexual

You partner's telling you they love you, does NOT make up for the harm they are doing to you. This is NOT love!

Do you feel as if you:

- Have to walk on eggshells around the other person, to avoid doing anything to upset them
- Are acutely conscious of monitoring what you say to avoid conflict
- Second guess yourself and worry more that you're not saying the right words
- Have to apologise for their behaviour

If so, then you'll already have an idea that something is amiss, although you won't necessarily want to admit it. Oftentimes, the fear of being without them, in those initial days, weeks, and months, is scarier than the thought of staying in the toxic situation.

In some relationships, these red flags can be moderated with counselling and help, straight away. However, if they are left unchecked, there is a high chance that the relationship will become even unhealthier and could head down the destructive path of abuse.

Listening to your intuition is vital to helping yourself, and acting upon it is even more important. Generally, the next stage along a toxic path leaves you unable to stand up for yourself at all, and fearful of saying or doing anything that might aggravate the other person—so you don't. At that stage, you have already—unknowingly—begun to learn how to be submissive and are being conditioned to their control.

There are already many—millions worldwide— who feel trapped and who don't know how to overcome that paralysing fear, to escape. They are looking for ways not only to survive but also to escape and thrive.

The effects of domestic/family violence are equally serious for the survivors: families, children, and communities.

Survivors can face:

- Fear
- Lack of trust
- Depression and mood swings
- Shame
- Guilt
- Anger
- Drug and alcohol abuse (to numb the pain)
- Suicidal thoughts
- Injury
- Self-harm
- Anxiety
- Death

Witnessing or experiencing domestic/family violence can have a damaging effect on children.

Children in toxic situations can:

- Feel guilty that they are to blame for the violence
- Show behaviours such as, aggression, low self-esteem
- Show physical reactions, such as bedwetting, headaches, and stomach cramps
- Withdraw from friends
- Encounter problems with schoolwork
- Be bullied or become a bully
- Use drugs or alcohol
- Self-harm
- Grow up, without learning about positive relationships (especially if they have been in an abusive household for an extended time)

If you are worried about a child who is in a toxic situation and who may be in danger, contact your local child protection agency. It is important that they get the support they need. Ensure they have access to someone they can talk to like Kids Helpline.

And let's not forget the impact domestic violence has on the people around the victim and the communities they live in.

Families can face:

- A breakdown in the way the family functions
- Household conflict
- Frequent moving house, to avoid the abuser
- Upheaval and involvement from the authorities, such as police and child protection

Abuse is generational. It's a learned behaviour that is passed from generation to generation. We aren't born abusers, just as we aren't born racists. However, some people believe abuse is normal behaviour, because they don't know any other way. When communities turn a blind eye to domestic violence, they allow it to continue.

In a relationship, you should be able to communicate safely with the other person and allow your voice and opinions to be heard. It's about respect and how you respect other people's opinions in a safe and reasonable debate.

How do you know if your relationship is healthy?

The following points are signs of a healthy relationship, or are things that enable a happy relationship to flourish:

- You can trust your partner easily and don't need to question them
- Your partner likes your friends and encourages you to spend time with them; your partner wants to include them in both of your lives
- You make all the important decisions together
- Your partner understands that it's normal and healthy for your relationship, when you spend time away from them, and they don't question you about it
- Your partner doesn't put you in situations where you have to lie to protect their reputation or cover for their mistakes
- Your arguments are handled fairly, using facts not emotional attacks
- Your partner encourages you and helps you reach your goals in life

- Your partner likes you for who you really are, not just what you look like
- You partner doesn't pressure you into doing things you don't want to do
- You and your partner show respect for each other
- You often talk about your goals and your feelings about your relationship
- You are not afraid to say what you think and why you think that way
- You like to hear how your partner thinks and don't always have to agree with them
- You both feel you have a friendship and a physical attraction
- You don't need to be with your partner 24/7
- You don't need to check your partner's phone or check on their every move, because you have trust
- You feel as if your relationship is based on equality, open communication, and respect for boundaries, as well as trust and, ultimately, commitment

A healthy, well-functioning relationship makes you feel supported and connected. You feel independent, but still feel well-connected with each other. A healthy relationship has safe communication, trust, boundaries, and mutual respect. Communication is most important, as is setting healthy boundaries. If you disagree or argue with your partner, you need to feel safe about voicing your concerns. A violence-free relationship is a healthy relationship.

Your relationship should bring more happiness into your life than stress. Ultimately it's about happiness. YOUR happiness! Every relationship will have problems and stress, at times. You need to remember that this is your life and you need to prevent prolonged mental stress. Self-preservation is about bringing more happiness into your life and taking care of yourself. Ultimately, it also about having great self-esteem and maintaining your self-respect.

Imagine a life that is free from drama and stress at home! I mean, I know there's no such thing as a perfect partner or a perfect life. However, imagine if you felt that you could truly rely on your partner for support, without the fear or anxiety associated with a toxic person? Living in constant fear, anxiety and stress, takes its toll on your health; both mentally and physically.

The women I've spoken with have told me that they feel broken to the core. They feel completely depleted and empty inside. They feel completely exhausted all the time, and as if they are merely keeping up appearances. They don't know how to change their lives.

I know it's not easy; it's never going to be easy. But it is possible. It can get better and it will get better. You can change your life.

It starts with you. Your life is important too. You were not born to be miserable or sad. You can make your own life better. You matter; but, you have to take responsibility for your life, no matter how difficult it is to face.

Self-preservation is also about your ability to take care of yourself. Let's take a closer look at the warning signs, which might be worryingly familiar.

CHAPTER 4
The warning signs

Sometimes, people who are in toxic relationships, or suffering from domestic violence, don't see the red flags or don't want to. Living with constant fear and anxiety is like a shadow you cart around with you every day and you become accustomed to it. You fall into patterns, which become second nature, such as automatically apologising in every text, phone call, or for every noise or disruption. It's common for women to apologise before anything has even happened.

Domestic violence doesn't care what age you are, how much money you have, how nice a person you are, what job you have, or where you live—it happens too often and all over the world. It's an unacceptable violation of another human being.

As a community, we can keep an eye out for this type of behaviour and not condone it by ignoring it or enabling it. Instead we can voice our concerns about it and check in on the victim(s).

Consider paying closer attention to someone who displays these behaviours:

- Ridiculing or publicly humiliating another person
- Making insulting comments about someone's body, personality, religion, or beliefs
- Threatening to publicly disclose things someone has said or done in private
- Showing jealousy and making condescending remarks about someone's family, friends, or pets

- Intercepting another person's mail or telephone calls, to monitor whom they are in contact with

- Consistently claiming to know the 'right way' to do things and how, where, and when things are to be done

- Interrupting another person's work, time spent with their family and friends or activities they enjoy, in order to get their own needs met

- Putting pressure on someone, with sexual connotations (lewd remarks, inappropriate touching, forcing another to engage in or watch porn, or other sexual acts)

- Forcing someone to apologise for things they haven't done

- Name-calling in public

- Interrogating someone about their whereabouts

- Making unfounded accusations of you being unfaithful or lying

- Threatening suicide

- Demonstrating their ability to cause physical harm by damaging property
- Using intimidating body language
- Blaming everything that goes wrong on another person.

These are all indicators of a potential abuser trying to gain control over someone else.

It's not easy discovering your 'normal' life is anything but normal, and that you are living in a domestic violence relationship. However, acknowledging that you are is the first step to changing it, and to removing yourself from it. It's important that you reach out to the community of friends and family around you, and accept the help and support that's offered.

Here are some questions for you. Do you:

- Have less contact with your family and friends than you did before you entered your relationship

- Discourage people from calling you, or don't pick up the phone at home, because of your partner's jealousy, mood, or behaviour about your spending time with or speaking with someone other than them
- Feel uneasy about being with your partner and your family and friends at the same time
- Change the way you are/act differently around your partner to appease them
- Feel nervous or fearful of what your partner will say or do if you come home late from work, shopping, or visiting others
- Speak carefully or avoid speaking at all, so you don't risk upsetting your partner
- Feel guilt or shame about doing anything at all for yourself
- Compensate for time by doing other things, so you can be accessible or do things your partner wants to do every day
- Take your children out of the house to get them out of the way, or to avoid the negativity or drama of your partner

- Put everyone else, including yourself, last so you can cater to the demands of your partner
- Do extra housework or yard work just so you don't need to ask them to help or do it, so they don't get in a mood about it or take it out on you somehow?

If you said yes to any of these, then please be aware that they are alarm bells. None of them are ok, and it's definitely NOT ok that you feel any of them. Deep down you know that this is not how a relationship should be.

The stress that the above puts on your mental and physical health may eventually show up in the form of:

1. Anxiety

You might feel anxious and fearful about making your own decisions, and guilty about not seeking approval beforehand.

2. Fear of a 'blow up'

The apprehension that you are going to make your partner angry, because you are voicing your concerns or opinions, is a terrifying fear, which can make you feel isolated and anxious. You may feel as if you are constantly gauging the atmosphere, and trying to keep the peace, by giving in, keeping quiet, or avoiding 'inflammatory' topics.

3. Panic attacks

Sometimes fear and anxiety can take physical forms. Panic attacks, where you might have difficulty catching your breath, have a pounding heart, and feel sick or faint can be a result of extreme anxiety. Panic attacks can happen anywhere, at any time.

4. Self-doubt, lack of confidence and a sense of worthlessness

Domestic abuse diminishes your sense of worth, as well as your freedom, and increases your damaging dependence on your partner. Ultimately, this might lead you to feel as if you're not good enough, and that you deserve to be hurt or mistreated. You might become so confused about the truth that you feel as if you are going crazy.

5. A marked change in personality, or withdrawal from family and friends

You may be prohibited from seeing your loved ones or you might separate yourself from family and friends, because of self-esteem issues, or the fear of your partner's reaction. Sometimes your entire personality changes noticeably; e.g., a formerly outgoing person becomes withdrawn, overly serious, or quiet, and has difficulty making eye contact or looks at the ground while talking.

6. Depression, thoughts of suicide

Over long periods of time, physical and emotional abuse can have a severe impact on mental health. Depression is common amongst victims of domestic violence, especially if sexual abuse has also occurred. Thoughts of suicide are also common, with studies showing that around 20% of domestic violence victims have considered taking their own life.

It's important to be aware of this and to look at all of the above, to understand what is normal and what is not. Sometimes, it can be difficult to know when a behaviour crosses the line; from a healthy to an unhealthy one or even to abuse.

Look at the following list of warning signs, to help you recognise whether your relationship is going in the wrong direction:

- Do you feel as if your partner constantly checks your phone or email without permission
- Do they constantly put you down?
- Do they exhibit extreme jealousy
- Does your partner have an explosive temper
- Does your partner isolate you or make false accusations about you
- Does your partner have mood swings
- Are they possessive towards you
- Does your partner pressure or force you to do uncomfortable things that you disagree with?

As you can see, there are plenty of warning signs to be aware of. However, you need to be completely honest with yourself, if you are to realise the truth. Sometimes it's difficult to face the truth, when it's clouded by your perception and judgement of your current situation. The warning signs can also be clouded by the other's person's perception of reality, which they reflect onto you. At this point, you may even feel as if you're sacrificing your life and that you don't have a choice or a voice to be heard.

The truth always prevails. Your warning sign might be that little voice in your head, which keeps telling you 'this feels wrong. Or that pain in your stomach, which aches when you feel so very sad about your life and your current situation.

Warning signs and red flags can often appear when alcohol is involved. Alcohol enables the other person to lose their inhibitions and disables their ability to put on a 'perfect partner' act. They let their guard down and show you their true nature. Alcohol and drugs can cause major problems in relationships, as they fuel the fire and lead to many arguments and disagreements.

Something to be aware of, in the early stages of a relationship, is that scenario where your partner 'always manages to get into a fight at the pub'. Someone's true nature and personality often appear when they are drunk or under the influence of drugs.

However, drunk or not, there is no excuse for bad behaviour, abuse is still abuse!

CHAPTER 5
Use your intuition, good vibrations

Your intuition is one of the most powerful gifts you have been given. Your gut instinct cannot be explained, but it is something that comes at you with an obvious force and intention. Everyone has heard of using your intuition, but what does this really look like? How do you tap into this invisible force, which is designed to guide you through your life in a self-preserving, helpful way, to keep you safe?

Human beings experience intuition on many levels, some very powerful. The instinct to save your life is the most powerful and the most important. Feel that powerful force, deep down in the pit of your stomach. It could save you from serious injury or even save your life.

It is really important to trust your intuition. This subconscious energy speaks to you well before your physical body and brain have even had a chance to process what is going on around you.

Imagine you are walking down a street and you see someone walking towards you from the opposite direction. You instantly feel uncomfortable. Why do you feel so uncomfortable? What are you going to do? Do you keep walking directly towards that person, knowing your alarm bells are going off, or do you follow your instincts and walk in the other direction? You instinctively have a choice to walk away from that 'negative' energy. That is called using your instinct and it is your intuition of self-preservation.

Where does that voice in your head come from? Why do we experience intuition? They are both very important components of self-awareness. Knowing why you sense those instinctual feelings can be like an epiphany or a revelation. These messages from the universe are there to guide you through life, usually during the most threatening moments of your life.

Knowing when your partner is cheating on you is another example of using your instinct. If you've been in an unfaithful relationship before, you'll know the feeling. You had a gut feeling that something wasn't quite right. You felt this sickening feeling in the depths of your stomach that your partner was with someone else. You felt an overwhelmingly uncomfortable energy, which almost made you want to vomit. You felt as if a piece of you was broken to the core. I first experienced this feeling as a teenager. It struck me that the universe was sending me a message, directly to my gut.

How can just a simple feeling or intuitive thought create such pain, anxiety, and anguish? It's totally unexplainable, but it's true. This is intuition operating at its highest capacity. Our thoughts are so powerful that they can create physical reactions. Your own energy is deeply connected to your 'other person's' energy, and as soon as that energy is altered, somehow, you feel the shift in an unexplainable way.

Should you trust this voice in your head? How do you know it's actually true? What if it's all in your imagination? Well, your body reacts in an undeniable way. Your body is directly connected to your brain and your thoughts are directly linked to your intuition and instinct.

We have all received signs—in life—which, if we looked closely enough, were loud and clear! Those warning signs came through the universe and they were messages for your soul.

Trust your innate wisdom, this higher voice, as these are universal messages! Your instincts know what is going on, long before your mind has caught up. When your mind does catch up, you'll have one of those OMG realisation moments … You can't fake intuitive feelings. Your soul is in tune to your intuition and knows when something is not right.

Keep in mind that your truth is only your truth. It might not make any sense to anyone else, however your heart knows what is true. Trust your feelings, as this is your life. Deep down in the depths of your soul, your heart is at peace.

Try not to discredit or doubt your gut instinct, as these messages and feelings are important. You might feel as though you're becoming paranoid. It's ok to doubt the feelings, if you believe you can trust your partner or the situation around you. However, it's incredible how our bodies can pick up on bad energy and bad vibrations.

Vibrational energy is an energy field which is an unexplained force. You always hear about good vibrations and positive vibes, etc. Even science has confirmed that everything in the universe, including you, is pure energy, which is vibrating at different frequencies. That might seem a little overwhelming, but it's mind-blowing when you think about it. Life is so infinitely precious and fragile, and being here is a blessing. Life is a gift; a miracle and we must embrace it and appreciate it.

It's interesting to take note of what energy is around you and how different people can make you feel. You feel uplifted when you are around positive people with positive energy and high vibrations. You also notice that when you are around negative people with negative energy, you feel drained, sad, deflated, or flat.

Sometimes, if you want to feel good about yourself, you need to make a conscious effort to surround yourself with positive people, who have positive energy! I call them glass half-full people. You cannot create a positive life, with negative energy around you. You cannot hang out with negative people and expect to live a positive life. This statement is profoundly life changing!

Observing your thoughts and feelings, regularly, is important for your mental health. Negative thoughts lead to negative experiences and lower our vibrations, and you feel bad as a result. Positive thoughts lead to positive experiences and raise your vibrations, resulting in feelings of extreme happiness and joy.

I was always brought up to be positive. Positive thoughts are imperative for a happy life. I call it being the eternal optimist. No matter how bad the situation, you are in, there is a lesson to be learned, a blessing in disguise, or good to be found in the bad. It's so important to stay positive, no matter what is happening around you. Be grateful for the lessons and pain you have suffered in life (more on this later). Stay positive always. This is self-preserving behaviour. Practice positive thoughts and look for positive vibes. Always be present in the now.

It takes practice to live in the moment; in the now. It takes practice to pivot your mind towards positive thoughts, particularly if you are a pessimist by nature. It is possible though. Start with daily gratitude. It will change your thought patterns, which I'll discuss a little further along.

CHAPTER 6
Judgement

As human beings, we tend to be particularly judgemental when it comes to how we perceive other people, as well as other people's decisions and lives. Why are we so harsh on each other? Where does this judgement come from? Why do we feel the need to be such strong critics of other people—especially strangers—about whom we know nothing? More importantly, how does it impact us and corral us into making decisions that are not necessarily good for us?

Your home, your car, your hair, your skin, your walk, your talk; the company you keep; the way you dress or parent, the way you do literally anything—it's all judged by someone somewhere. Judgement has happening since the dawn of time. It's ugly and every one of us can't stand it, but it happens, right? I always say, judge me when you are perfect, and I mean, there's no such thing as perfect.

Judging is a very poor habit we all need to work on kicking. Generally, it stems from a lack of self-love. Judging a person always defines who you are, not who they are. But, what I want to talk about more is YOU judging YOU! Judging yourself can erode your soul, your self-esteem, and your confidence, leaving you vulnerable.

Our harshest judgments always come from ourselves. It can be crucifying! We are most definitely our own worst enemies when it comes down to it. We worry about things that might never happen, and we spend far too much time wondering what everyone else is thinking about us. This consumes too great a part of our day—doing it, and worrying about it. It's all based on our perception of how we 'think' other people should be living and it stems from ego and a lack of self-love. Trust me when I say, that focusing on your positives is a much better use of your time, and goes a long way to helping you feel courage and confidence.

When there is self-love, there is compassion and ultimately less judgment—period.

For generations, society has judged separated or divorced women in particular. I was talking to a close friend, just today, who is separated from her husband. She spoke about the judgement she felt as a newly-solo mum. Once she was no longer part of a couple, and was juggling small children, invitations to parties, dinners, and get-togethers decreased. She was seen differently, and sometimes even seen as a threat to other friends' marriages, simply because she was single.

Remember; sadly, no one is spared from being judged. Even a married mum will be judged! Think about that for a minute. How many times have you been out, maybe at the supermarket, and seen a mother trying to wrangle a screaming toddler's tantrum? Married or not, the faces of those around the mum quickly show whether they empathise with or judge her. Mostly these opinions originate from beliefs that we have learned along life's journey, however the voicing of them stems from ego.

The fear of being judged can keep you in a holding pattern of survival, in even the worst scenarios, simply because you don't want anyone judging or thinking poorly of you. Amazingly, it's this fear that sometimes puts people's safety at risk—when they stay in toxic and abusive relationships.

You're judged if you go, and you're judged if you stay–so, you may as well do what's best for you and your children anyway. The sting of judgement is only temporary and like a mosquito bite, it irritates for a while and then you eventually forget about it. No-one else has the right to make your decisions for you. Whatever you decide, it's no one else's business but yours. If you make your choices, based on other people's judgments, you will always find yourself making the wrong ones.

Here's what I want you to know. You did your best, you're doing your best, and you will always do even better with the gift of hindsight, foresight, wisdom, and education.

Surviving a toxic or abusive relationship bleeds you of everything, and the last things you need any less of are self-love, self-worth, and self-confidence. Remember that those, who make you feel less than you really are, THRIVE on that control. You don't need to believe it and, furthermore, you don't need to believe other people's judgments of you, full stop.

Do they really know the real you? Do they understand your circumstances? Do they understand the dynamics of your relationship? Do they see, feel, or know what it takes to SURVIVE your current life, everyday?

I'm guessing not, and if they did, they would be quick to help, not quick to judge. So let's focus on you and what you pin on yourself.

Being single isn't something to be feared. Understand that you are on this journey for a specific purpose. Your journey in life isn't the same as someone else's. Your purpose isn't the same as someone else's either. This unique life that you call your own is to be lived to your greatest capacity. It can be frightening and scary, however it doesn't' need to be feared.

Imagine you had the perfect life; well, you thought it was perfect. As with most relationships the honeymoon period is normally blissful and you're giddily in love. Then, fast forward a few months, a year, maybe a few years, and you're married and maybe you have children. You're a married couple with two kids in private school, and an unlimited income etc.

When you want something better for yourself and your children, the universe conspires to help you take the action you need to make a change for the better. However, change can be challenging. Oddly enough, the fear of the unknown is sometimes more frightening than the fear of the known. Finding yourself in new territory, as my newly-single friend did, is going to rattle you for a week or longer.

The uneducated (about your life) will judge, probe and treat you differently. The best thing to do is to prepare yourself for it. Don't fear it. You may no longer feel 'normal', or a part of the group you used to see, once you're a solo or a single parent. If you didn't work before, maybe you need to now.

Guess what, someone somewhere will judge you on that too! But there's nothing wrong with a woman or man getting out there, and doing what they need to do, to get closer to the life they want and deserve. Let the haters hate; you have more important things to do than tie up your time with a fake view of your life.

Here's something important to consider: when you make choices based on others' judgements, you're making a choice for someone else and not yourself.

Here's a question for you: how can you live YOUR life, your best life, and find your purpose, when the choices you make are based upon another person's life and not your own? The short answer to that is that you can't. You'll end up leading a false life. You'll be being walking to the rhythm of someone else's drum. You'll end up feeling as if something's missing and you'll be on the money—something is missing: YOU.

The choices you make are yours and yours alone.

Get yourself ready for a total transformation. Doesn't that excite you? You are about to become who you are REALLY meant to be.

The real, authentic you! When you are that real you, you'll find it's effortless, and you feel happy, you feel full, and life flows.

Do you want that?

Do you think you deserve it?

Do you BELIEVE you can have it?

I hope you answered 'yes' to all of the above, because it's very doable. You just need to decide. I hate to tell you, though, that when you do get it done, and you're living your best life, someone will still judge you. Yes, as I said earlier—they will judge you anyway!

Let them whisper, while you flourish, because those kinds of people will eventually exit your life. Then, you'll have space to attract and welcome new friends, with whom you can breathe, be yourself, and have the conversations you've longed for. You'll feel the immense relief of being in a space that is authentically and naturally you. You'll no longer be fitting into someone else's ideal of who you should be etc. No, you'll no longer be just surviving; you'll be thriving and LIVING!

CHAPTER 7
Addicted to love

There are many types of addiction! Coffee, alcohol, drugs, chocolate, social media, mobile phones, gaming, technology etc. Addiction is a part of our lives, whether we admit it or not.

Addiction is a behaviour which creates a pattern that can either be healthy or unhealthy, depending upon the positive or negative impact it has on your life! If you are addicted to walking, meditating or going to the gym, for example, it's healthy for you! If you are addicted to having a bottle of wine or two every night, then that's unhealthy for you and can be negative on your life.

Having an addiction often helps people to escape reality. If your life is a painful reality, where you suffer, you intentionally want to numb the pain and escape to a place where there's no pain or suffering. An alcoholic blur softens the harshness of a life you don't want to keep enduring. However, having an addiction can bring embarrassed feelings and make you feel ashamed of the choices you make. As with most addictions, it can totally rule your life and dictate how you live it.

Every choice you make in your life can greatly affect others as well. It's easy to fall into an addiction, but very difficult to escape from one. Does that sound familiar? Changing habits and removing addictions from your life can transform your world and give you a happier, healthier state of mind, body, and soul.

The human brain is addiction-prone (not minimising it any way) and you need to make sure that, when you are ready to change your life, and remove the toxic thoughts/addictions from it. You can replace these with healthy thoughts and healthier habits. These will be far more beneficial for your well-being, and the well-being of your children and future generations!

I bet you didn't know that if you're in a toxic or abusive relationship, then you're in the high risk category of being addicted to love! We're not going to cue Richard Palmer and his girls in their little black dresses and slicked back hair, because it's serious!

Love is addictive because it makes you feel incredible! When you first meet your partner, the feelings of euphoria wash over you like a spell. You get swept up in your own love bubble and everything else, including a good amount of reason goes out the window! It's a chemical reaction in your brain, which floods your physical body with endorphins—the happy hormones—so you feel completely overwhelmed with happiness. Love is a rush of strong and positive feelings. Both emotionally and mentally, it fills you with hope and positivity.

No one is immune to falling in love. It takes over your emotions and mental state like a trance, which can't be broken. If you meet someone who is potentially toxic, they will most likely love bomb you with all sorts of text messages, romance, and flowers etc. You may even feel as if they are smothering you with love. During the initial stages, though, you'll see it as a positive thing. Your self-esteem will be high and you will feel amazing, up on Cloud Nine!

After the initial infatuation drops off, the relationship moves into the next phase. This is where you get really comfortable with the other person. For a healthy person, this is a loving caring relationship where conflict can easily be defused by an open discussion, which takes place in a safe and healthy way. Your partner will listen to you and not get angry when you voice your opinions or thoughts.

Sometimes, you start to feel uneasy with your partner after a while, and something doesn't feel right; but, you brush it off because you're addicted to the feeling of being in love. You put love above all else: reason, logic, and common sense etc. This is because there is a notion that everyone should experience a fairy tale love! You deserve to feel it, right? If you are female, you dream of one day of marrying your Prince Charming and living happily ever after. You are in LOVE with the idea of being in LOVE. Love comes first—love is forever and ever.

I always talk about the idea of loving yourself more, if love is finally lost and your relationship comes to an end. Imagine a mirror in front of you and you are holding all of the love that you wanted to give to someone. Imagine giving that love to yourself and feeling that euphoric feeling about yourself. It takes practice and focus, but it's an important way to practice self-love.

Everyone has an idea of what a perfect relationship should look like. If you feel as if your partner should love you more, then maybe you really need to love yourself more. By loving yourself, you boost your self-esteem and confidence. Fill your own cup up with love. You will find everyone else will still feel loved as a result, they may feel even more loved by you.

Are you addicted to the thought of being in love? Is that why you self-sacrifice for your partner? It's a complex issue, and not loving yourself enough—as crazy as that sounds—is possibly the reason why you do this. You want to love your partner more than yourself, because you are crave the ability to LOVE another person, because it makes you feel good. What if you were to love yourself as much as the other person? Would this make you feel the same euphoria? Are you making excuses and accepting the other person's faults because of your ideals of love; because of your addiction to the idea of being in love?

CHAPTER 8
What if you decide to stay?

What if you stay?

We've spoken about leaving a toxic relationship. Now, I want to discuss the idea of staying. What does that look like?

What if you want to do every single thing you can to make the marriage work—for the sake of the kids and for keeping the family together? This is the most important decision of your life. You are at the end of your tether and you just want some help.

You might feel as if you are damned if you do and damned if you don't. You might feel powerless and as if the only chance you have for your relationship to survive is if your partner gets help.

So, your partner needs to get counselling and you both get marriage counselling. Counselling is the best option to pivot your relationship and gives you the best chance for both of you to move forward. This can be quite a stressful time. You might feel exposed, telling someone else about your dirty laundry. You might feel anxious about being honest in front of your partner, and fear that they will bring it up when you are home alone (or any time they get a chance to use it against you). You might feel as though you have no options left. This is the make-or-break moment. You need to try everything; you must not let down the kids. There are many reasons and they are all your own.

Some people use seeking help as an ultimatum, to try to save their marriage. Usually, you need to book quite far ahead to see a marriage counsellor/psychologist. So you will need to convince your partner that this is a make-or-break situation. You must let them know that are at your wits' end and you can't go on anymore. If communication has completely broken down, sometimes a text message is the safest way (you might think) to communicate without a blow up.

So, you might finally convince your partner to go that counselling session, where you can get advice on how to communicate, as well as ideas on how to improve your relationship. You are hopeful that things can change and that your partner will implement all of the new relationship boundaries etc., to make the relationship work.

If you choose to stay it might feel as if you are going around in circles. You might think you are always having the same conversations and arguments with your partner. Your frustration will be building, and every time you have an argument, you may very well feel as if you are going back to square one.

Imagine you are in a boardroom and you have to make a business decision. I want you to imagine your partner with you in the boardroom, and try to keep the emotion out of the room when you are discussing issues. This is a very helpful tip, as females tend to be emotionally reactive. Your discussion with your partner needs to be based on how you are feeling, but you should try to keep emotion out of the discussion. This takes practice, because your partner might say something that upsets you, or they might criticise you. You need to keep your head screwed on tight, so you can think about what they are saying logically rather than being overcome by emotions, which can cloud your judgement of the situation.

Rational thinking takes practice but it helps when you're making major life decisions, especially about your partner. If you stay, you'll need to ensure you are making the right decision and that you won't have any regrets. It's not until you stay that you realise that you might have to make compromises and sacrifices, to keep your partner happy and to ensure the relationship is balanced. If they feel as though you have too much power and control, then you might find yourself having more confrontation and arguments with your partner.

If you stay and your relationship is healthy, then you might be able to make it work.

If you stay and your relationship is unhealthy, then you might find yourself feeling as if you are suffocating. You might find that you stay because your partner continually promises to change. You want to believe that they will change; you love them after all. What if they do change? How long are you going to wait to find out whether they can change? How many chances are you willing to give them and how many slip ups are you wiling to forgive them for?

That is entirely up to you. Every person and relationship is different. However, in many of the couples who go through marriage counselling, the partner promises to be different and to change. Some may eventually change, but others won't. Self-preservation is about how long and how willing are you to stay and to keep going. You are the only person who can decide how long you stay.

If there is no abuse in the relationship, then you may be willing to do what ever you can to make your relationship work. Forgiveness, date nights, quality time together, and learning each other's love languages; these are all ways to reconnect after a breakdown in the relationship. If your partner broke the trust in the relationship, it is an extremely difficult thing to come back from. It is very difficult to get trust back, but if you go to counselling you might be able to learn techniques to help with this.

Weighing up whether you should stay or go is your decision. No-one else can tell you stay or to leave. It's entirely your decision, but I know you will want to do everything you can to make it work. It's good to know you've done everything you possibly can to save your marriage.

But, you must remember that it's only going to improve if both parties are willing to compromise and to change. You need to weigh up how much of your own individual happiness you are willing to sacrifice, and how much possible suffering you can endure.

CHAPTER 9
Power and control

What you need to remember is that, regardless of what kind of abuse you or anyone is facing in life, the core of it is all about control.

The ultimate goal of a person who uses abusive tactics, such as physical, emotional, spiritual, sexual, or financial abuse, is to gain power and control over another. Most abusers wear their victim down, in order to feel that power and control. It is just as common for people to experience subtle forms of abuse; such as, emotional, psychological, or financial abuse, as it is for them to experience obvious forms of abuse; such as, physical or sexual violence.

Most abusers will use a range of abusive tactics, in multiple categories, to try to gain power and control.

Threats, threats, and more threats! The most common forms of domestic violence are threats of physical and sexual assault and actual assault, although it is usually the actual actions that make others aware of the problem. Although an abuser may only assault another physically, once, they may then use that one assault to instil the threat of future violence, in order to gain control over the assaulted person's life.

The Domestic Abuse Intervention Program (DAIP) created the Power and Control Wheel, overleaf, in 1984. It outlines some examples of the abusive tactics that are used to gain power and control. I've shown it to many people, over the years, and they can't believe how insightful and revealing this diagram is. It's confronting to look at, especially if you are experiencing this cycle of power and control.

There is a pattern to abusive behaviour—called the Cycle of Violence—that shows victims how to recognise that they are in an abusive relationship and to determine which part of the cycle they are currently in. From the women I've spoken to, when you're in the thick of abuse, you may think it's a temporary or a one-off thing. It's not always clear that you are caught in the pattern of your partner's behaviour. Once you actually sit back and observe that pattern, over a period of time, you will definitely see a cycle, similar to the diagram on page 90.

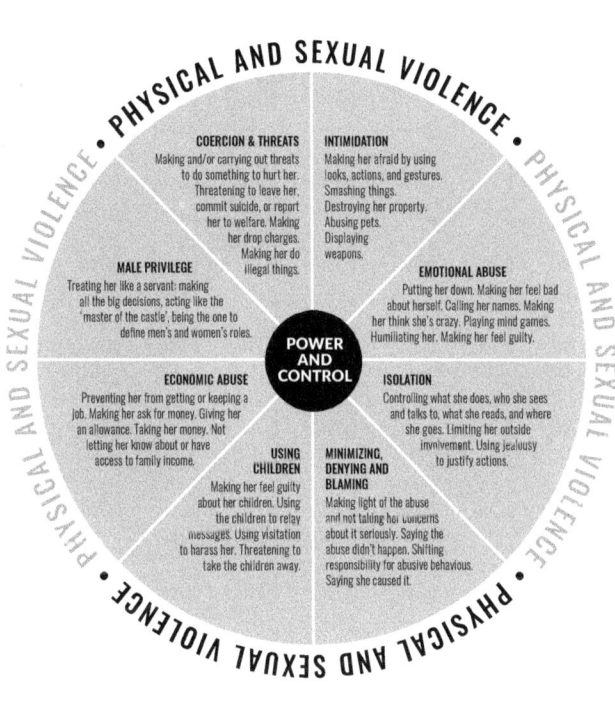

Power and control wheel

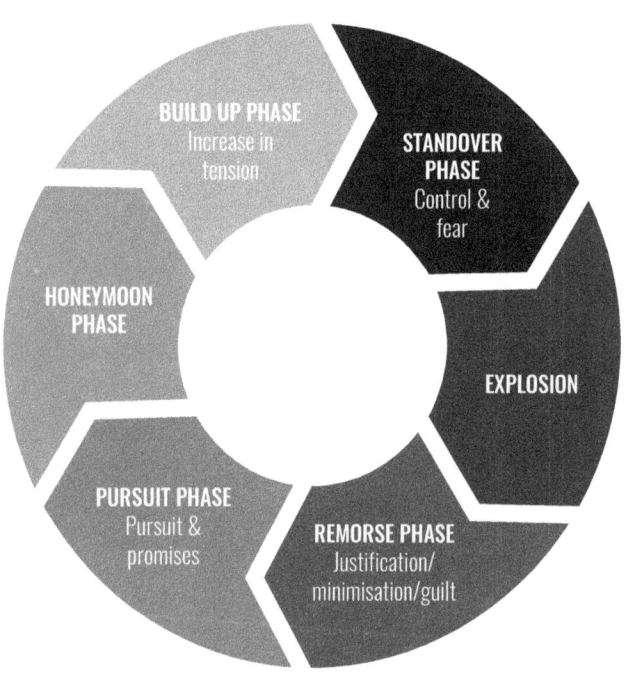

Cycle of violence

This might all be pretty confronting for you; but remember, you may be a victim now, but you can be a survivor tomorrow!

The Australian Bureau of Statistics reports that:

- One in five women has been the victim of violence from their partner
- One in four women has experienced emotional abuse from their partner
- A quarter of women do not report incidents of domestic violence
- Three out of four domestic violence homicide victims are women
- One woman dies, every week, at the hands of her current or former partner. (Australian Institute of Health and Welfare)

These statistics show how appallingly widespread violence in the home is in our society. Even more shocking is how inaccurate these numbers might be, since many incidents of domestic violence are never officially reported to the authorities.

It's time to pop the bubble. If you recognise these behaviours, are feeling the effects of them, and can pinpoint where you currently are in the cycle of violence, you are doing WELL! Better still, you have recognised it and are ready to face it head-on.

This is your life, your happiness, and it's your right to live with freedom and to feel safe.

Why do we stay in bad relationships? What are the reasons behind our self-sacrificing behaviour?

There are many reasons, which is why many find it so difficult to leave.

All too often your abuser will tell you that no one will love you like they do. They will strip your self-esteem to nothing, so that when they say no one else could put up with you, or that no one will ever want you, you probably believe their lies; falling for the deception of abuse they constantly dish out to you.

They'll use whatever means possible, to keep you under their control, including heaping immense guilt on you about your children and saying that the children need them. This tactic specifically shames you into not even considering leaving, as it coerces you into believing their world would fall apart if you did. Some abusers take it one step further, by threatening to take your kids or money away. Some say they will commit suicide, if you ever leave them, or they make threats of violence against you or the children.

The cycle diagram on page 90 mentions the rollercoaster of threats followed by apologies, to reassure you that they will change and be a better person. It's one you'll see over and over again, if you stay in the abusive relationship, because the abuser just can't stand to lose their power or control over you.

Even knowing all that you do, it's not easy to leave. You come up with a thousand excuses to stay, and constantly risk your well-being, because you haven't developed the confidence to leave.

Do any of these excuses sound familiar?

- I don't have the financial resources, or know-how, to be financially independent

- I love him; we have so many good memories I hold dear
- If he can be as amazing as he was when we first met, surely this is a phase and he'll be that incredible man again
- The kids need their father/mother; he's/she's a good provider and parent
- I don't want to break up my family unit
- I'll just wait until the kids get older—I don't want them going through the upheaval
- I don't have anywhere to go—I feel embarrassed to flee and be seen as dramatic
- Marriage is forever, I feel as if I've failed.

There are many reasons why people feel trapped and choose to stay. The most common of these are the history of good memories with your partner, the feeling of nostalgia, and the HOPE that things will get better, over time. That can happen, for a tiny percentage of relationships, but you can't count on it. That is an unsafe solution for something that is better tackled with space and support, particularly if you have children.

Domestic violence's impact on children is enormous. If you are torn between leaving a toxic relationship and staying for the kids' sake, then leaving sooner rather than later will have LESS impact on your children, in the long term.

Children, who witness domestic and family violence, are at risk of facing higher levels of behavioural and emotional challenges than other children do. The impact of their abusive environment varies from child to child, depending on their age, sex, and role within the family.

Children from environments of domestic violence may exhibit the following behaviours:

- Copying the abusive or violent behaviour
- Sleeping difficulties, i.e. nightmares
- Trying to intervene and stop the abuse
- Being stunned into a terrified silence by what they've witnessed
- Blaming themselves
- Feeling frustrated, angry, or depressed
- Bullying others or being bullied
- Being cruel to animals

- Regressive behaviours, such as bed-wetting or thumb-sucking
- Being nervous or withdrawn
- Changes in behaviour and low academic performance at school
- Displaying sudden unexplained conditions such as headaches, tummy aches, asthma, or stuttering
- Running away from home
- Attempting suicide or self-harming
- Abusing alcohol or other substances

As a parent, seeing any of these signs in your children can be totally heartbreaking, but remember, there are numerous support agencies and resources available, which specifically help adults and children who have been in domestic violence environments to make the transition safely.

- Be aware that domestic and family violence harms children too
- Educate your children that there is never any excuse for abuse and violence

- Provide reassurance that the abuse and violence is not the child's fault
- Make sure your child knows that he or she is loved—tell them daily
- Organise support at school—talk to a teacher, principal, or guidance officer
- Encourage the child to talk about their feelings
- Seek support with counselling
- Ensure the child knows the emergency number, '000' ,and how to seek this help
- Seek support via the local domestic and family violence service or the state-wide 24-hour service (details are in the back pages of this book)

Your children are your number one priority. However, society has conditioned us into believing that children need two parents. Women are caught between a rock and hard place, when deciding whether to leave an abusive partner. Becoming a single mum or a divorcee can bring a lot of guilt and shame with it, and being a full-time mum doesn't allow you to return to work to support your children. It is a difficult situation, often made worse by drugs and alcohol, which cloud people's judgement and ability to make logical decisions.

The final reason we stay is fear; either fear of physical violence or fear that the abuser will commit suicide. These are the two most common reasons why abused people stay in these situations.

All forms of abuse are damaging. A person's confidence, self-worth, and self-respect can become greatly depleted, and that impacts their thinking and their ability to seek help and enable their self-preservation. Emotions are intense and feelings of depression, sadness, confusion, guilt, frustration, anger, helplessness, and powerlessness are all part of the reasons why we stay.

Ultimately, though, it's fear... the fear of telling someone you are leaving and the consequences that will follow. You ask/tell yourself:

- That no one is going to listen or believe that you have a problem
- How are you going to cope alone
- How are you going to support your kids on your own
- If you leave, the problem is only going to get bigger, so why leave
- If you stay, the violence is going to escalate, and they are only going to get angrier

These are the main reasons why we feel trapped in the cycle of violence. The only way to break the cycle is to leave it, but that is not as easy as it sounds. However, it is possible and it can be done—carefully.

BREAKING FREE OF TOXIC RELATIONSHIPS

CHAPTER 10
Preparing for freedom

It's so important that you have a plan in place, to prepare you for what is going to be an emotional rollercoaster. You are in a fight for survival. You need to be mentally tough and physically prepared in every way possible.

Never underestimate the level of danger you may be in, particularly if you are planning to leave an abusive relationship. Please make sure you stay safe. This is THE most important thing—your safety and the safety of your children!

Your safety plan

The following tips can assist you in developing a safety plan for you and your children:

- Know and talk to your trusted support person—the one you are going to lean on and be in contact with, after you leave. Go over your safety plan with them so someone knows what's happening and can call the emergency services, on your behalf, if needed. Add emergency numbers into your phone such as 000 for police; DV Connect 1800 811 811 (24/7 crisis line) and your primary support person.

Consider where you will go for safety, such as family or friends or a Women's Refuge—somewhere your partner won't suspect you'll be. This is important. Don't make it your best friend's house or somewhere obvious. It needs to be somewhere secure, with security gates if possible, or with a high level of security.

- Plan to take your children with you. It's important that you remain calm with them.

- Prepare an emergency bag that includes money, spare car/house keys, and copies of important documents (e.g., birth certificates, passports, and school information for the kids, in case you need to change their school), medications, marriage certificate, and clothes. Remove them from the house and give it to your support person for safe keeping, in case you need to leave quickly.

- Plan how you will leave in an emergency situation, i.e. travel by car, bus, train, family, or friend(s).

- Consider getting another phone, with a different phone number that can be used after you leave. Give the school and other important contacts this number so you don't need to read messages or answer the phone to your partner, until you're safe and ready for that. Leave the new phone in the care of your support person or the place where you'll be going.

- Consider your postal and banking arrangements and open alternate accounts.

- Change your postal address to a friend's or another family member's postal address.

- Carefully consider what information you share on social networking sites.

- Don't go posting your plans or any pictures of locations all over social media, which can be recognisable for tracking you down. Your security and privacy is paramount at this time. The best course of action is to stay off the internet, until the heat of the situation passes. Change ALL your passwords the day before you leave or that day.

- Educate yourself about community agencies that can assist and keep their numbers handy. There are plenty of community support groups to contact. There is full list at the end of this book. Put the contact numbers in your phone.

- Discuss your safety plan with your children. Make them aware of what might happen, so if you do need to leave they know what the safety plan is. You need to be cautious here, young children should not be told, as the responsibility of keeping that information private would be too great. It is advisable to ask a support agency about this.

- Delete all recent phone numbers and texts you have made in case your partner decides to snoop on your phone. Also clear all website browser information on all devices.

- Teach your children how to place an emergency call to 000 in the days leading up to your leaving.

- Review your safety plan with police or a local domestic violence service counsellor. Give them the new phone number so they have access to you.

~ Inform trusted family and friends of your plans— they may assist as needed. Again, be cautious here. You need to tell absolutely as few people as possible at this point and only those you know you can trust 100%.

Checklist of what to take when leaving

Financial

~ Bank account details—online banking is good; make sure you have all of your details saved on your new phone.

~ Money—have some money put aside in a separate bank account, in your name, or give some money regularly to a relative or friend so they will have it ready for you.

~ Credit cards—take credit card statements with you or open a new credit card account with a different address

Legal documents

~ Any court papers, including protection orders/family law papers

~ Passports

- Marriage certificate
- Lease/rental contracts
- Mortgage and property deeds
- Medical records
- School records
- Car registration papers
- Insurance policies
- Divorce papers

Identification

- Your driver's licence
- Children's birth certificates
- Your birth certificate
- Centrelink cards

Other

- House and car keys
- Medication
- Jewellery
- Photographs

- Children's toys
- Clothing for you and your children
- Current unpaid bills in your name

Preparing yourself mentally

It's normal to be afraid. It all seems overwhelming, but it's important that you are mentally prepared.

Some women can be so afraid that it can take years before they leave a toxic relationship. It's normal to feel trapped and vulnerable, but there is support for vulnerable women in these relationships, and you will be able to leave eventually. It's a choice you need to make for your own self-preservation and, if you have children, it's for their safety as well.

It's normal to feel some form of shame, when you leave. Shame is an unpleasant, self-conscious emotion that is associated with negative thoughts about yourself. Feelings of distress, exposure, mistrust, worthlessness, and powerlessness are also common feeling together with shame.

Leaving looks different for all of us...

Something might finally snap within you, and you decide to leave without telling anyone. This is understandable, but be careful about not having support people arranged to lean on. Your friends and family will be there to support you, even though you may feel as if you are a burden.

You might need to persuade your abusive partner to take time out from your relationship. I call this defusing the situation by saying you are taking a break from each other, to make it sound less dramatic than breaking up entirely. Soften the blow and break the news more gently, by saying you need time to work on yourself and to find yourself again. It might be that you need to tread more lightly for a few weeks or even a few months.

Going under the radar is important. What does this mean? It means you need to try to remain as normal as possible, and to go about your daily life, without showing your intention to leave. Keep to your daily routine and try to pretend that everything is as normal as possible.

CHAPTER 11
Keeping yourself safe

Your safety is paramount, when you decide to leave a toxic relationship. You need to remain as calm as possible during this stressful time. You will be feeling anxious and nervous, so it's vital you look after yourself. Take some time off work, if you need to; your work will understand. You just need to let them know what is going on, so they can support you.

Even though this can be an extremely stressful time, you need to make sure your own safety and the safety of your children and immediate family are always at the top of mind. Make them all aware of what is going on, so they can do everything to support and protect you.

You need to stay hypervigilant and alert, as you might be in a vulnerable position, after your ex-partner loses control of the situation. You've seen all the statistics; however, you need to be mindful that you or your children are more likely to be harmed in the first **48 hours after leaving**.

There might have been an incident, where your partner physically abused you and you were forced to call the police. The police may put a Domestic Violence Protection Order (DVPO) in place, so you are forced to leave the relationship. Follow the police's advice, if you are in danger. (There is a more detailed explanation of the DVPO a little later in this chapter).

Staying safe after separation

Here are some suggestions that may help you to remain safe after your separation:

- Consider taking out a Domestic Violence Protection Order—for support contact your Regional Domestic & Family Violence Service
- Keep copies of any current or new DVPO, on your person
- Make copies of any DVPO and provide them to:
    - Family, friends, and/or neighbours
    - Your children's day care or school
- Discuss your safety concerns with family, friends, and neighbours and encourage them to phone the police, on your behalf, if needed
- Stay in touch with your Regional Domestic and Family Violence Service
- Stay in touch with the police for information and advice on DVPO breaches
- Consider reviewing your bank and mailing details
- Arrange for caller ID on your home phone
- Consider changing, or making mobile or landline phone numbers secret

- Where possible, vary your routine, i.e. change the day you shop and the supermarket you normally use. Change your route to and from work or the children's school
- Speak with your employer about your DVPO and request your phone calls at work be screened
- Consider seeking legal advice for all family and property matters
- Make certified copies of all important documents
- Increase your security at home, i.e. change the locks, install sensor lighting, and use dowel rods in your window tracks
- Contact the Australian Electoral Commission, and request your name and address be suppressed on the electoral role
- Consider your internet safety, i.e. information you share on social networks, e.g. Facebook
- Carefully consider deactivating GPS devices on your mobile phone, computer programs, or the internet.

There is a possibility that things will escalate, as soon as your partner gets the slightest indication that you are leaving the relationship, because they will be losing control of you. At that point, there is a huge threat to your safety and the safety of your close family members and your children. That is why it is so critical to put a safety plan in place **first**.

Staying safe, if things escalate:

Here are some suggestions to help you remain safe, if things escalate before you can leave:

- Stay as calm as possible
- Be aware of where your children are
- Where possible, move to a safe area or leave the property
- Consider avoiding rooms with weapons, i.e. the kitchen, bathroom, or garage
- Be aware of rooms where there is no exit
- Follow your safety plan
- In an emergency, call the police on '000'.

Note: The Police have the authority and a responsibility to remove an abusive person to a watch-house, for four to eight hours. Additionally, they can make an application for an urgent Domestic Violence Protection Order on your behalf.

What is a Domestic Violence Protection Order?

A Domestic Violence Protection Order sounds like a scary process, but it's essential for your own safety. This is a legal document—It is a civil order, made by the court that restrains, restricts, and prohibits the behaviour of your ex (called the Respondent on the document) towards you (the Aggrieved) to prevent further domestic and family violence. The DVPO also imposes conditions on the Respondent, to prevent domestic violence from continuing. If a DVPO is breached, and reported to the police, charges may be applied and the Respondent can be charged in a criminal court.

This is an extremely important document and process, for your own safety, as scary as it sounds. You might feel guilt or ashamed about this process, as well, but keep in mind it's vital for your own protection.

How do you get a Domestic Violence Protection Order?

There are two types of Domestic Violence Protection Orders (DVPO):

- Police Application—Police complete the application on behalf of the Aggrieved
- Private Application—The Aggrieved completes the application.

If you're considering a private application, it is recommended that you seek assistance from the police, court staff, Legal Aid or the Regional Domestic & Family Violence Service. Application forms can be obtained at your local Magistrates Court or can be downloaded from the Department of Communities website under Forms and Factsheets. Legal Aid QLD also offers useful documents such as Your Legal Options Explained, which can be found on their website.

Responsibility and authority of the police

The police have responsibilities and authority under the Domestic and Family Violence Protection Act 2012, and Police Powers and Responsibilities Act 2000.

These acts enable the police to:

- Enter a place (with force if necessary) to investigate a domestic violence incident
- Detain a respondent and to take them to a watch-house for four to eight hours
- Make an application for a DVPO on behalf of the Aggrieved
- Demand the name and address of any person involved in a domestic violence incident, including witnesses
- Provide additional information about potential criminal charges that the Aggrieved may consider
- Provide information and referral to other domestic and family violence crisis services

As much as possible, stay off the alcohol to keep your wits about you and your mind as clear as possible. Try to stay in constant contact with a close friend or relative, and make sure you tell them your whereabouts at all times.

Take some time off work and try to break your daily routines, so your ex-partner won't know where you will be getting your morning coffee from, or when you might be at the gym etc. Stay off all social media, so you can't be traced to your location. You might want to change your passwords on email and social media accounts. Always log off when you're finished! Be mindful of what you post online and ask your friends to do the same. Ask them not to include you or your kids. These are simple things that will keep you under the radar for a while.

Don't answer calls from unknown, blocked, or private numbers. Change your voice message, so your name is not included, or use a pre-recorded voicemail message. Change your postal address to make sure you can't be traced.

If you have kids, take them out of school for a mini-break, if you can. If you must continue to take them to school, make sure you let the teacher know what is going on, so they can support you and the children as well. Children may feel torn between their parents, so it's vital they are aware that your decision to leave has been made to keep them safe and healthy. Make sure you ask the school to update your emergency contacts.

Be aware that your parents may also be targeted at this stage. Your ex-partner might contact them, to try to reach you or get to you through them. Be aware this is very common and it can be a stressful time for your parents. Please make sure they are aware of your situation, so that they can also take the necessary steps to keep themselves safe after you leave.

I know it all sounds overwhelming, but you really do have a choice. You have a voice and you need to understand that your own safety and that of your children come first.

People might say it's only a piece of paper, but a Domestic Violence Protection Order is so much more than that. It's a legal document, which enforces the law and ensures your safety, the safety of your children and your immediate family, if they are listed on the document. It's important to ask for help, if you need support. Don't be afraid, be strong and you will get through this difficult time.

CHAPTER 12
Your support network

You are NEVER alone. You ARE NOT to blame for your partner's violence.

Let's have the conversation about the police. Many people are afraid of them. They can be intimidating and scary in their gun-accessorised uniform, but I want you to know that if you are strategic, the police can become your newest best friends.

Our police service is mandated to protect and support you! They are there to serve the community and to bring offenders to justice. You may need to change the way you think about the police, because they are there to support you during the most challenging and difficult times in your life, when you are at your most vulnerable and your life is most at risk.

Make sure you know that it is you who has the power – you who changes everything. You need to believe in yourself. It is NOT ok, if someone is hurting you or threatening you. I know it's hard to maintain your self-confidence and self-control, but it's NEVER ok to feel unsafe in your own home.

Your health

At this point, the most important thing is your health. Go to your doctor and talk to them about your situation. Tell them you need to see a counsellor, so you qualify for a mental health plan of free counselling sessions. Your counsellor will also be a support person to whom you can talk in confidence. Know that they will listen and not judge you or your situation, and will give you the important support you need at this difficult time. Your doctor will also liaise with your counsellor to ensure that your safety remains paramount at all times.

Once you have seen your doctor, book in to see the counsellor. It is extremely important that you have the support you need, and are mentally tough and resilient, so you can prepare yourself to make the best decisions for you and your children's future.

Ensure you change your address and phone number with your doctor and your counsellor as well.

Finding support

Don't be afraid of the police, they are there to help you in this situation, which will be taken seriously.

For all EMERGENCIES call the Police: 000

For all non-emergency reporting and enquiries call Police Link: 131 444

For personal enquiries about your case or DVPO, call your local police station

More contacts are in the back pages of this book.

Remember this important information: make your plan and keep it where your partner won't find it.

Legal support

See a solicitor—get legal advice

Another important thing you can do, to protect yourself, is to get legal advice. Find out where you stand, legally, as it concerns your home, your finances, and all of your assets. You should always get legal advice before you make the move, because it can give you the information you need, as well as the confidence to feel completely ready to make the move.

A family lawyer is the best person to contact, or your local community legal centre (legal aid) if you can't afford a solicitor. Make an appointment to see a solicitor, as soon as you feel you need to leave your unsafe relationship. They will empower you with the information and support you need at this stressful time.

The most important message, here, is make sure you put a plan in place. Use the check-list from the safety plan. It's crucial to your safety and the safety of your immediate family and children. Stay alert and also be aware of your partner's movements, so you can protect yourself and your children.

Note these helpful support resources down somewhere safe, even under an alias, if you have to, such as your best friend's mum's name. That way it doesn't raise any suspicions.

Here are some very helpful support resources which you can lean on in times of crisis.

- **1800RESPECT** – 1800 737 732 - https://www.1800respect.org.au/https://www.thehotline.org/
- **Lifeline** - https://www.lifeline.org.au/get-help/topics/domestic-family-violence
- **Lifeline tool kit** - https://www.lifeline.org.au/static/uploads/files/domestic-violence-tool-kit-2012-wfnbsmivtcix.pdf
- **Mensline** - https://mensline.org.au/
- **Red Rose Foundation** - https://www.redrosefoundation.com.au/www.safesteps.org.au
- **Scope** - https://www.scopedv.org/
- **White Ribbon** - https://www.whiteribbon.org.au/

Make sure you use the support of friends, whom you trust. Don't feel as though you will be a burden on them. They will be there to support you, just as you would for them.

Be honest with your family, also, about the situation you are in. They will understand and be supportive of you and your children, where they can. I know you probably don't want to burden them; but, you might be surprised just how supportive and strong they will be for you during this difficult time in your life.

If you have children, contact their school and tell them what is happening. Speak with the school's guidance counsellor about the impact on your children and the support they can offer your children while they are at school.

Surround yourself with positive, uplifting people, who encourage you to believe in yourself and build your courage.

HEALING AND LIFE AFTER A TOXIC RELATIONSHIP

CHAPTER 13
Healing

So, you've faced your greatest fears, gathered up the courage, and left the relationship or marriage you thought would last forever. You've decided that your life is valuable and you are worthy of happiness. You've taken back control of your life and are allowing your self-preservation mechanism to take over.

Being true and honest with yourself is very empowering. However, it's also quite uncomfortable to face, when you're at the lowest point in your relationship. There is hope though.

You will grow through this process of grief and adjustment and become stronger, which will allow your soul to soar. You will empower your spirit with the true essence of who you are and attract amazing friendships and wonderful experiences into your life. Being vulnerable is being alive. You are only human and feelings come and go like clouds in the sky; however, if you live by the rules of the self-preservation guide, you'll be on your way to living a full and happy life again.

Ultimately, it starts with you. You are responsible for your own health and well-being. As soon as you take responsibility for yourself you'll be empowered with strength and self-belief.

Let's go back to that dreadful word, 'grief'. You need to grieve for the life you once thought would be forever. You need to grieve for the ex-partner you thought would be 'the one'. You need to grieve for the future life you had all planned out in your head.

We all go through grief differently, but here is some accepted wisdom, to understand about grief.

Grief

To understand grief is to live it. We are human beings, going through a journey, and grief and loss are unavoidable experiences of life. Whether it is the loss of a loved one or the loss of a relationship, every person grieves differently.

You may feel denial and isolation, where you try to alter the reality of the situation and to isolate yourself from the truth. This is a temporary response, which helps you cope with the first wave of pain and suffering.

Then you might feel anger, which can manifest itself in many forms. The pain you are feeling is enormous, and your natural instinct is to be angry. You can feel anger at your expartner, for hurting you, and anger at your family, friends, and the world in general, because you've become a victim of grief. It is human nature to blame those who have hurt us, in an effort to defuse anger. Anger and even aggression are natural reactions to being hurt, but these emotions also protect you from the possibility of being hurt again.

The next stage is bargaining, where you try to regain some form of control of the situation (if only I had of tried harder or done more).

Then there is depression, which is commonly associated with grief. The sadness is overwhelming and just getting out of bed can be difficult. Grief washes over you like a storm in the desert and you feel isolated, alone, and sad. Sad with your life and sad with your entire situation; you feel that no amount of counselling or chocolate will get you through it.

Eventually, you will come to terms with your situation and accept that the marriage is over, and you have to move on with your life. This is the period where you may feel withdrawn from the world. However, a calm feeling will follow and you need to allow yourself the time to just be. You have now surrendered to the situation and the universe is nurturing you. If you have a faith, or believe in God, then this is what will get you through this period. The strength of prayer is empowering. You will get through the difficult times and eventually appreciate your suffering as a blessing, because you have allowed yourself to grow and evolve.

Make sure you continue to see your counsellor during this time of grief. They can help you understand the emotions you are going through and can also explain more about your core beliefs. More information on this is listed below.

Establishing healthier belief systems

Your negative emotions are signals to value yourself more

The pain and hurt you have suffered, all throughout your life, build and build, including those of the relationship from which you have just escaped. These are called 'core hurts' and can best be described as vulnerabilities to your sense of self. They are different from just feeling bad, sad, anxious, or disappointed; they are when you feel bad 'about yourself'.

Some possible examples of core hurts might be when you feel, or suspect you feel:

- Disregarded, unimportant
- Accused
- Guilty
- Devalued
- Rejected

- Powerless
- Inadequate, unloved

Because of the great influence which core values have in building the sense of self, the deeper core hurts may sabotage or control your core values. There is more on this in the next chapter.

Doing the healing work on yourself essentially prepares you and sets you up for your new life, free from fear and guilt.

At this time, it is very important to your comeback - to be around your support network. It may even inspire others to do the same, and to come back into your life.

CHAPTER 14
Core Values

Core values are those things you believe in, no matter what; that you live by despite everything; that make you 'you'.

Core values can be lived in many great ways—when we help people out of danger, make a strong connection with someone, see great beauty in a work of art, have a spiritual experience, or become aware of our own humanity.

In order to reconnect, or strengthen your connection with your core values, ask yourself the following questions (the answers may take some time to become clear):

- What is the most important thing about me as a person?
- What is the important thing about me as friend/ partner/ parent?
- What is the most important thing about my life in general?

You might find it helpful to ask those people, closest to you or who know you well, to help you remember what your core values are and to reconnect with them.

It is important to understand that a stronger connection with your core hurts = a weaker connection with your core values. This leads to your thinking, feeling, and acting in ways that are not in accordance with your core values and beliefs.

A weaker connection with your core hurts = an increased connection with your core values. This leads to your thinking, feeling, and acting in ways that honour your core values and beliefs.

Your core values manifest themselves frequently, on a daily basis in fact, as a subconscious motivation to improve, appreciate, connect, or protect. Doing any one of these things automatically activates your core values. Do whatever you can to improve, appreciate, connect, and protect your partner, your relationships, your family, and your friends. This strengthens your connection with your core values and weakens your connection with your core hurts.

In Chapter 13, Healing, I spoke about how the core hurts, i.e. the pain and hurt which you experienced in the past, can have a powerful effect on your present life and relationships. At the same time your deeper core hurts can control the top ones. What this means is that you can become trapped in a cycle of resentment, pain, and abuse, which seeks to repeat itself. You end up feeling as if you 'deserve' to be in an abusive relationship, because of your sense of low self-worth.

I often recommend Dr. Steve Stosny's amazing book, 'Love Without Hurt', to people. Steve is a qualified psychotherapist and the founder of CompassionPower. He was inspired to write this book by his work with couples and individuals, who were suffering from all forms of resentment, anger, abuse, and issues of violence. In his book, he explains all the many different types of abusive relationships, to help his readers recognise where they are in their relationships. Most importantly, he teaches compassion, as a tool for self-healing and looks at ways your partner might use compassion to rewire their own anger, resentment, and abusive behavior.

Not surprisingly, researchers have found strong links between those suffering from clinical post traumatic stress syndrome and those exiting abusive relationships. The following quote is from an academic study into the concept of posttraumatic growth, and I believe it applies as well to exiting and abusive relationship—certainly a traumatic experience!

'Post-traumatic growth or benefit finding refers to positive psychological change experienced as a result of the struggle with highly challenging life circumstances... Post-traumatic growth is not simply a return to baseline from a period of suffering; instead it is an experience of improvement that for some persons is deeply meaningful. .. This concept is part of the positive psychology approach. It is commonly reported by cancer survivors.'

(Tedeshi and Calhoun, 2004)

History

Even though the researchers, above, were writing in 2004, people actually realised, thousands of years ago, that suffering and distress can bring positive changes. The early writings of the ancient Hebrews, Greeks, and early Christians, as well as some of the teachings of Hinduism, Buddhism, Islam, and the Baha'i Faith, all speak about the potentially positive life-changing power of hurt (suffering).

Think about how pain and suffering, and how characters overcome them, have been the central theme of novels, plays and poems, ever since man and woman was able to put pen to paper. What would have become of Elizabeth (or Bridget Jones, for that matter!) and Mr Darcy's relationship, if he had not been able to overcome his own arrogance, unhappiness and prejudice?!

I spoke earlier about post traumatic growth (PTG)—that is—the way things can improve after you overcome a traumatic experience. This has been well-documented in relation to various traumatic events, such as life-threatening disease, war, abuse, immigration, and the death of loved ones. Studies of different countries and cultures have also found evidence that, although PTG is a universal phenomenon, it has cultural variations' (Linley and Joseph, 2004). In the study I quoted earlier, the researchers also said that they discovered 'overwhelming evidence' that people, who face very difficult circumstances and who experience significant change in their lives, often view these changes as 'highly positive' (Tedeshi and Calhoun, 2004).

So, no matter where trauma occurs, researchers agree that it is not only possible for individuals but also for families to grow from overcoming their trauma (Berger and Weiss, 2008).

Causes of PTG

No pain, no gain. How many times have you heard this? Ask any athlete, and they'll tell you that winning made all the sacrifices, pain, and injury of training worth it. Well, it will be the same when you start your new life. The pain and sacrifices you experience and make, when you leave your abusive relationship, will be worth it.

It's not the fear and the unpleasantness of situations that cause PTG. Rather it is the individual's 'struggle with the new reality in the aftermath of trauma that is crucial in determining the extent to which posttraumatic growth occurs'(Tedeshi and Calhoun, 2006).

Encouragingly, reports about people who experienced growth after overcoming a traumatic event far outnumber reports about those who suffer ongoing negative effects. However, it doesn't 'just happen' as a sort of bonus. It requires some pre-existing circumstances.

Some of the factors that have been associated with positive growth following trauma are:

- Spirituality – research has shown that those with (or who have developed) spiritual beliefs experience PGT more often then those without

- Social support – is a well documented buffer against mental illness and the stress response
  - There is even some evidence to suggest that social support helps decrease our brains responses to stress (in the Hypothalamic-Pituitary-Adrenocortical (HPA) Pathway in the brain (Ozbay 2007)).
- Therapy/counselling – the opportunity for therapy where you can work through your emotions, both negative and positive, (emotional disclosure).

As I have stressed throughout this book, abuse can happen to anyone. So, it is not surprising to learn that studies showed that neither gender processed trauma better. Of course they experienced various gender-related traumas, but overcoming these was mutually beneficial to all genders.

Characteristics

Post-traumatic growth is not the same thing as resilience, hardiness, optimism, or a sense of coherence. It refers to a change in people that is greater than the ability to resist being damaged by highly stressful circumstances.

PTG means that you move beyond the way you felt, before your trauma and change. It makes sense. If you have always been someone who coped with everything that was thrown at you, then you may not notice a lot of positive change, after recovering, as you are used to it and have developed coping strategies, over time.

What this means is that feeling you are not prepared and feeling apprehensive, or even downright terrified, means your gains will be bigger too! Discovering that you can leave your situation and cope with the associated trauma, over time, could make you stronger than you have ever been.

People who have experienced PTG display some of the following characteristics:

- Greater appreciation of life
- Changed sense of priorities
- Warmer, more intimate relationships
- Greater sense of personal strength
- Recognition of new possibilities or paths for one's life
- (Increased) Spiritual development.

Two personality characteristics that may affect the likelihood that you can make positive use of the traumatic events that you have experienced are extraversion and openness to experience. Being optimistic helps you to focus your attention and resources better on the most important matters. It also helps you to disengage from uncontrollable or unsolvable problems.

Your ability to grieve and to accept the trauma that you have experienced can also increase the likelihood that you will grow. Part of that grieving and acceptance may come from talking to those who supported you. They can help your PTG by offering you an outlet for talking about the changes that have occurred, in a way that helps you to make sense of them. They can also offer some perspectives that you can use to move forward, instead of looking back.

It's not going to happen overnight, and everybody copes in different ways. Take it one step at a time and imagine that every change you make—no matter how small—is a step on your journey to a much bigger change. Don't lose confidence in yourself, but think about how having faith in yourself will eventually get you that life you want.

Finally, know that even though you might be feeling low, this is actually another step on the path to PTG! It is possible to have negative thoughts at the same time as you have newer, more positive ones, and your grief and sadness can be the starting point for your positive response.

It is important to understand why we behave the way we do. Sometimes our behaviour enables others to treat us badly and allows that bad behaviour to continue. This is a very important clue to understanding why we stay in bad relationships and why we continue the cycle of domestic violence.

This information, along with therapy, helped my friend rebuild her relationship with herself and to understand what she wanted her future self and her future life to look like. She wanted to value and honour herself with her core values.

It is the same for you. You are NOT to blame for another person's bad behaviour. However, if you don't change your pattern of thinking, you are enabling others to continue treating you in a toxic and unhealthy manner.

If you can learn to have some self-respect, with core self-values, then you will not only be honouring your own true potential but you will also show your children how they should treat one another. It's as simple as that.

You are in control of your thoughts, which control your behaviour and your actions. If you change your thoughts, you change your behaviour, which demonstrates to others that you are living your life with self-respect and honouring your core values. This is self-preservation.

CHAPTER 15

Building your new life

It's time to look towards the future and a happier you!

It is important to have a Personal Empowering Mission Statement. We do them for companies, so why not ourselves?

However, remember, everybody is a 'work in progress'. Go easy on yourself. Don't beat yourself up about the mistakes and choices you have made in the past. Grow and learn from those, to make your future how it should be.

Your Personal Mission Statement

What is a personal mission statement?

You are capable of so many amazing things in your life. It all starts with you. When my friend left her situation, she changed her thought patterns and moved into the next stage of her life. I encouraged her to write a personal mission statement to remind and guide her.

It looked something like this:

- I promise to forgive myself for all of the past
- I promise to forgive myself for not loving myself or treating myself with respect
- I promise myself I will never be treated with disrespect
- I promise I will never allow myself to be spoken to or treated in an abusive way

- I promise myself I will always consult with my close family and friends, if I am unsure of the decisions I make regarding a new relationship
- I will never allow myself to get involved in an abusive relationship again
- I promise to love myself and my children first
- I promise myself to always follow my gut instinct, my heart and my head when making decisions for my future
- I promise to follow my core values

Developing your own self-respect personal 'Mission Statement' is powerful. Try it for yourself.

Here's another example of a mission statement, based around finding the right partner. This is something you can look at, when you think about your future self. Yours might be about finding the right job or making the right decisions concerning you.

Mission Statement

I've done a lot of soul-searching.

I am a sensitive, caring, loving, and kind person.

I am an open book; no games, gimmicks or manipulations with me.

I am looking for those qualities in my partner.

I am looking for someone who is emotionally available and who loves me for who I am; not who they want me to be.

In the past, people have taken advantage of my kind nature and giving heart.

Now, I need someone who is not afraid to show me how they really feel about me, and who feels comfortable about themself.

I need someone honest, who is spiritually connected to me on a deep level; someone I can trust with my life.

Someone who can be my best friend and soul mate, but have as much respect for me and my opinion, as I will have for them and theirs.

I am a loving person and I have endless love and energy to give the right person, who loves me the same in return.

I will never allow myself to make a bad relationship decision, without thinking logically and discussing with my family and closest friends.

I will not apologise for who I am, and I will follow my instincts and trust myself.

I don't have to prove myself to anyone anymore.

Core values

What are your core values? Imagine you are at your own funeral. How would you like people to remember you? Here are some examples of words you might like people to use about you:

Dependable, reliable, loyal, committed, open-minded, consistent, honest, creative, positive, good humoured, compassionate, spirit of adventure, motivated, optimistic, passionate, courageous, perseverance, service to others, and environmentalist.

Make a list your five top core values.

Who do you need to surround yourself with for the best chance of recreating your life in a positive way? You already know the answer to that! Your positive friend, who lifts you up, or that crazy relative who always makes you laugh.

Be in tune with your gut instinct to avoid having toxic people in your life. Use self-respect and self-preservation to give yourself permission to live your life guilt-free. Break free from the patterns of the past. You have been stuck in a situation where you were going around in circles, and now it's time to break the cycle. You are in control of your life. Now—more than ever—there is support out there. Use that support to give you the tools you need to create the better life you deserve.

Embracing new ways of thinking also includes new healthy patterns of doing things. Being physically active, in some shape or form, is vital for your body and mind. When you exercise and move your body, you convert your stress into your strength. Endorphins are the happy hormones, which make you feel authentic happiness. Join the gym or ask a friend to walk with you. It's always nice to catch up over a walk.

Just think of this:

Strong Body, Strong Mind

Walk in nature for half an hour, take a nice swim in the ocean, or go for a run, to create new healthy habits. There are many ways to exercise, so do what works for you. Yoga and meditation are very helpful as well. Your body loves to stretch, and yoga is fantastic for stress relief. It takes time to feel the benefits, but it is worth the effort. Your body will thank you! Most importantly you are practising self-care and that is about prioritising yourself and your own health. You are practising self-respect and self-preservation.

Team sports can also be highly beneficial to your physical and mental health. By moving your body in a way you enjoy, you are exercising and focusing your mind in a positive way. For me, tennis is a moving meditation, because by focusing on what I am doing, I don't allow other thoughts to come into my mind. This can be said for any sport; so, go out there and give it a go. You will laugh, enjoy yourself socially, and reap the many benefits of playing sport.

Self-affirmations are an important part of your healing. Using them on a daily basis helps to build confidence. When you wake up in the morning and look at yourself in the mirror (it's pretty scary sometimes) I want you to say to yourself, "I love you!"

By doing this you are giving yourself permission to love yourself and you are accepting yourself, with self-awareness. Learning to look at yourself and say, 'I love you' can be daunting. We all have so many doubts about ourselves and engage in so much negative self-talk. We are more judgemental and critical of ourselves than anyone else is.

Be aware of negative self-talk (everyone does it). Acknowledge that it's just a thought and it will pass. I recommend constantly monitoring your negative thoughts. Just observe them and don't let them affect your presence. It takes practice, but it's important that you are in control of your mind. If you can control your mind, you can change your life. It's that simple.

Instead, pay attention to your inner voice of positivity and your optimistic thoughts. These thoughts are powerful enough to build your confidence, regain your strength, and get your mojo back!

Music is another important rebuilding tool that you can use. Music can help you heal and rebuild your life in a positive way. Music says what cannot be expressed in words. It soothes the mind and gives it rest; it heals the heart and makes it whole; it flows from heaven to the soul. Music will also enable your mind to feel soothed and relaxed. In times of stress and heartache, music can be your best friend. Take some time out to put your earphones in and listen to something relaxing, such as Bliss or Deva Premal. Then, there's what I call Abba Therapy! I turn Abba up really loud and instantly feel as if I'm in a happier mood! It's incredible what Abba Therapy can do for our souls!!!!

There's something else that can help you enormously; sunlight. Vitamin D is such an important vitamin, which is best taken as every day safe sun exposure. Studies have demonstrated the many health benefits of vitamin D.

In addition to vitamin D, make sure you are taking a multi-vitamin supplement and looking after your health. It's imperative for your self-preservation that you remain physically and mentally healthy.

Eating organic foods (where possible), can restore and heal your body from the inside out. One of the most important things you can do for your health is to eat fresh, locally-grown, organic produce. We are what we absorb, so be mindful of chewing your food thoroughly and if possible, avoid drinking fluids during your meals to allow your body to absorb your food fully.

Smoothies are another simple way of practicing some self-love and helping you cope with stress. You can put a great deal into a smoothie and they can be so nutritious and healthy. Ingredients such as spirulina, organic protein powder, kale, spinach, flaxseed oil, coconut oil, magnesium powder, and super greens are all essential ingredients and help you maintain energy and overall well-being.

CHAPTER 16

Time to thrive

Acceptance and gratitude

When you look back on your experience, you will see it as a massive learning curve in your life. It was a time when you grew so much as a person and learned to ask for help and to say, 'No, I'm not doing this anymore!'

You are going to get your power back. It's not easy to ask for help, but you will finally feel that your true voice is being heard. You will be able to say NO safely, and your opinion will matter! No one is going to take advantage of your kind nature anymore! Enough is enough; it's time to regain your power.

Accept your situation with gratitude and move on. Be grateful for your experience and the lessons it has taught you. It helped you become the truest version of YOU!

Forgiveness

The power of forgiveness is liberating. Forgiving someone, who has done the wrong thing by you, is a sign of your strength as a human. It's not an easy thing to do. However, if you separate the behaviour from the person, you will be able to forgive the person and to acknowledge that they are human and that we all make mistakes. You can also recognize that it was their behaviour that was the problem.

Forgiveness will set you free from the past. By forgiving yourself, which is extremely important, you show compassion for yourself, and thereafter you will be able to show compassion for others. You are self-empowering with love. Forgive but never forget the lessons learned.

Gratitude

Every day we take small things for granted, such as the air we breathe, the water we drink, and the food we eat. We are truly blessed to live in a wonderful place called Planet Earth and we need to be mindful of the small things the universe provides for us every day.

By practicing gratitude, daily, you are unlocking the true secret to happiness. There is always something to be grateful, for no matter how difficult your situation. Practice gratitude and watch how your life changes in a positive way. Write down five things you are grateful for every day. Your happiness is directly linked to your gratitude.

Optimism

Choose to see the world through optimistic eyes. A positive attitude has proven to be one of the main attributes of people who live to over 100 years old. You can change the way you think about any situation, by choosing to be optimistic about it. Every challenge you are faced with, ask yourself, 'What opportunity can I take from this challenge?' and by allowing yourself to be open to positivity, your life will change in a dramatic way.

Being in the present

We are all time travellers. Our thoughts constantly drift back into the past and far into the future. We forget about the present, because we have a preconceived idea about how our lives should be and how they should turn out. These are based on our beliefs and the preconditioning of our upbringings. By staying in the present, you will allow yourself to be immersed by the power of now, and you will give your life much more depth and meaning, in every single moment.

Reconnecting with your inner calm and peace

Three-second breathing: breathe in through your nose for three seconds and out through your mouth for three seconds. Count the seconds aloud, use the second hand on a clock, or count slowly to four, so your brain learns and remembers what three-second breathing feels like. You can also try breathing in for three seconds and out for five seconds.

This controlled breathing tells the stress-response part of your brain—that produces adrenalin and cortisol (i.e. flight-fight-freeze)—that you are relaxed and safe, so it can stay calm. This part of your brain has developed to help you. It has no eyes to see or ears to hear what is actually going happening; it uses your thoughts and your breathing to tell it whether you are safe or in danger. Too much stress and anxiety can get it 'stuck on 'on", like a sensor light when there is nothing there. Your slow breathing will—in time and with regular practice—help this part of your brain to relax. After that, the 'thinking and planning' and the 'connecting and feeling' parts of your brain will also work better.

Breathe when you first wake up, and throughout the day. Punctuate your day with controlled breathing. Breathe when you go to bed at night. Breathe if you wake in the night, when you are driving, queuing, showering, and throughout the day, to build new neural pathways and to help your brain know you are safe.

Even when you feel calm, practise breathing until it becomes automatic. Then, when you want to stay calm, or when there is an invitation to stress or anxiety, your mind and your body will automatically know how to stay calm. It will know that this breathing means 'let go and relax', because that is what you have been training it to do.

Mindfulness

Be present in the moment. Have your mind and body do the same thing at once (if you are showering just shower, if you are walking just walk). It is experiencing all that you can in your body—what you can feel (touch), see, hear, smell, taste, and your connection with nature. It is having your mind be part of this experience and not off having its own separate life. It is expanding into acceptance—'It is what it is!' it is peace of mind.

Allow your observing mind—rather than your thinking mind—to be aware of all that you are experiencing in that moment. Being mindful helps give your mind a rest from being separate from your body, and it gives you a rest from the tyranny of the thoughts that endlessly go around and around. There are also mindfulness meditations that you can practise.

Thoughts and feelings

Thoughts and feelings are just words and pictures. They are not necessarily real. They are our mind's impressions of our experiences. Sometimes they are good to have, and other times it's good to let go of them. Thoughts and feelings can be signposts top show you the way, but not to drive you.

Challenge unwanted and persistent thoughts. Ask yourself:

- Is it true—what is the evidence? Is it absolutely true?
- Is it good—is it good for me to think this thought?
- Is it useful—does this thought serve a purpose?
- Does it disturb my peace of mind or support acceptance?
- How does having this thought affect me?
- What am I afraid will happen, if I didn't have this thought?
- Who would I be without this thought?

Over time, you can develop new neural pathways that encourage your mind to think the thoughts you prefer or choose to have. You can choose not to engage with, or believe, or 'fuse' with, thoughts that are not true; or that are true, but not good for or useful or acceptable to you.

You can also imagine the troubling or negative thoughts to the tune of a song ('Happy Birthday' or 'Twinkle, Twinkle Little Star') or in a funny voice (a particular cartoon voice). Try this and see if it helps the thought to be less demanding or intrusive. This process does not automatically make the thought give up and go away, but it does assist you, over time, to be more selective about which thoughts you want to keep/discard.

Feelings

Practise 'sitting with your feelings'; i.e. just sitting, observing, accepting, and seeing you feelings coming and going or staying. Expand this to an acceptance of feelings that you may previously have resisted or denied.

Coming home to yourself

Take a moment to recall a place where you feel most at peace with yourself—perhaps somewhere in nature. Enjoy this feeling; embrace and breathe in this feeling; connect with it (perhaps using a memento or a photo). Take time to visit this place, whenever you can. Remember to visualise this place and how you feel when you are there. This is a 'coming home to yourself' feeling; a feeling that can sustain you and nurture you and remind you of what is most of value to you—your core values.

'5 out of 10'

Imagine that 5 is your balance point. A point below 5 can lead to despair and depression; and above 5 can lead to stress, tension, worry, and anxiety. To stay a 5 become 'intolerant' of anything/anybody that takes you away from being a 5. Excuse yourself, in order to maintain your '5-ness'. Consider choosing 5 out of 10 as a priority in your life. Breathing, mindfulness, thought-challenging and sitting with your feelings can all help you maintain your '5-ness'. Pay attention to anything or anybody that starts to take you away from, or prevents you getting to, a 5. Enjoy being a 5!

Tree trunk

You might imagine or visualise yourself as the trunk of a tree—strong, secure, solid, and at home with yourself. We often find ourselves way out in the very tiny, fragile twigs and leaves at the very ends of the branches of our tree-trunk selves ... not a very secure place to be! Come home, and be the trunk of the tree.

Change takes time, practice and remembering. Take steps to make some small changes in your life. Make them as often as you can, until they become a natural part of your life. Build on these small steps (like scaffolding). Be willing to take small steps towards change. Start to notice, and then to let go of, expectations (should, have to, need to, ought to, can't, mustn't) and exchange them for hope, choice, and curiosity.

There is always hope. If you face the sun, the shadows fall behind you. Embrace your new knowledge as power. I know it's not easy, but you have support. You can take back control of your life and be happy again, like you've never thought possible. Your life matters! Your life is important!

AFTERWORD

When I first started thinking about writing this book, there were so many women around me who were going through challenging breakups and domestic violence. They all said the same thing. There's no book or information to support us on how to get through it or any practical advice on how to survive such a difficult situation.

That's when I thought, if I can help one person who needs help at such a stressful time, then I will be happy. I want to be able to share my research and the knowledge that I've gained through talking about this issue with other women.

Domestic Violence does not discriminate! It affects people of all ages, races, religions, and status.

"If you want something to change, you are going to have to change it yourself and do something you've never done."

Change is hard, unpredictable, and moves us out of our comfort zones. Our brains are continuously trying to seek stability and comfort; but, for years, we have been hardwired into the belief systems that we inherited from our parent's parents. Change is normal, and is part of the human evolution of growth. It enables us to feel vulnerable and to surrender ourselves fully to the universe.

Our hearts want to live free, without fear, and in a total abundance of love. We truly have an immense capacity to love ourselves and others. Change is the imposter in our lives. The universal current that flows through us is ever-changing and dynamic, and we must embrace this vibration as a blessing not a curse. By embracing it, not only do we grow spiritually but our relationship with ourselves and other humans also transcends to a higher form. This form is closer to authentic love and is the truest form of love, which embraces all living beings.

The process of writing this book has given me a clear insight into the way we try to self-sabotage our lives. This must stop. We have to stop pretending we are living a perfect life, when we are living a frightening existence. Now, more than ever, it is time to change your life and you are sitting in the pilot's seat.

It's ok to have days when you feel flat and as though nothing is going your way. Having those days is all about your attitude to your thoughts. If you are having negative thoughts, simply observe them and say to yourself, 'I no longer wish to take these thoughts on-board', and then let them go.

Each of us has our own story, or book to be told. How is yours going to end? Are you willing to make your self-preservation and self-respect a priority? Are you self-sacrificing. like my friend was? Do you know that you can be happy and live your life without fear?

I am proud of you for reading this and for taking the first step.

How do you want the story of your life to end? The choice is in your hands.

Be safe

x

K

THANK YOU

There are so many people I would like to thank. Firstly, my amazing parents; thank you for your love and support. I would not have had the strength and determination to follow my dreams without you both. My wonderful children, my son and daughter; you inspire me to be a better person every day. Thank you to my past counsellors, my psychologist, and my closest friends who have seen me at my worst and who have always been there for me, every step of the way. Finally, I send a huge thank you to my incredible husband, who is my true love and best friend.

FURTHER READING

Great books to read

The Happiness Trap, Dr. Russ Harris, Exisle Publishing AU

Love without Hurt, Steven Stosey, Ingram Publisher Services US

RESOURCES

Agencies & Support Organisations:

- 1800RESPECT - 1800 737 732 - https://www.1800respect.org.au/
- https://www.thehotline.org/
- Lifeline - https://www.lifeline.org.au/get-help/topics/domestic-family-violence
- Lifeline tool kit - https://www.lifeline.org.au/static/uploads/files/domestic-violence-tool-kit-2012-wfnbsmivtcix.pdf
- Mensline - https://mensline.org.au/
- Red Rose Foundation - https://www.redrosefoundation.com.au/
- www.safesteps.org.au
- Scope - scopedv.org
- White Ribbon - https://www.whiteribbon.org.au/

Professional support for women and children experiencing domestic and family violence on the Sunshine Coast is provided by:

- Centacare Family & Relationship Services Maroochydore - https://centacarebrisbane.net.au/
- SCOPE Program Gympie - https://www.scopedv.org/

Domestic Violence Services:

- Immigrant Women's Support Services 3846 3490 - http://www.iwss.org.au/
- Sunshine Cooloola Against Sexual Assault Service - https://www.laurelplace.com.au/
  - Laurel House (Maroochydore) (07) 5443 4711
  - Laurel Place (Gympie) (07) 5482 7911
- Centre Against Domestic Abuse - https://www.cada.org.au/
  - Caboolture Regional Domestic Violence Service 5498 9533
- Brisbane Domestic Violence Advocacy Service 3217 2544 - https://bdvs.org.au/
- Working Against Violence Support Service 3808 5566 - https://centreforwomen.org.au/

Crisis Services and helplines:

- DV Connect (24 hours) 1800 811 811 - https://www.dvconnect.org/
- National Sexual Assault and DFV Counselling Service -1800 737 732
- Sexual Assault Helpline (7:30am—11:30pm) 1800 010 120
- Child Safety 1800 811 810
- Child Safety After Hours Centre 3235 9999 / 1800 177 135
- Kids Helpline (24 hours) 1800 551 800
- Lifeline (24 hours) 13 11 14
- Parentline (24 hours) 1300 301 300
- Pregnancy Counselling Link 1800 777 690

Housing:

- Tenant Advice & Advocacy Service 5476 0555
- QLD Department of Housing 5475 9700
- Sunshine Coast Regional Housing Council 5454 2900

Police Prosecutions:

- Maroochydore Office, 63 Cotton Tree Parade, 4558, (07) 5430 9900
- Gympie Office, 30 Channon Street, 4570, (07) 5483 7640, 5480 1066, 5480 1078

Child Contact Arrangements:

- Family Relationship Centre 5452 9700
- Lifeline Family Dispute Resolution 5479 1600
- Foundations 1300 854 733
- Sunshine Coast Contact Centre 5479 6971
- Caloundra Court 5420 9000
- Maroochydore Court 5470 8111
- Nambour Court 5470 8755
- Noosa Court 5473 8400
- Gympie Court 5480 5488

Legal Information & Advice

- Legal Aid 1300 651 188
- Women's Legal Service 1800 677 278

- Aboriginal & Torres Strait Islander Women's Legal Services Ltd 3025 3888
- 1800 012 255
- Qld Indigenous Family Violence Legal Service 1800 887 700
- Sunshine Coast Community Legal Service (Maroochydore) 5443 7827
- Taylor's Legal (Gympie) 5482 1147
- Refuge & Immigration Legal Service 3846 3189
- Seniors Legal & Support Service (program of Caxton Legal Centre Inc.) 3214 6333
- LGBTI Legal Service (D&FV and Sexual assault/abuse) 0401 936 232

Sunshine Coast Police Stations:

- Qld Police (EMERGENCY) 000
- Police Link (Non-emergencies) 131 444

Other Services:

- Victim Assist 1300 546 587
- Child Support Agency 131 272

- Centrelink 132 850
- Welfare Rights Centre 1800 358 511
- Department of Child Safety
  - Caboolture Office - 5490 1000
  - Caloundra Office - 5420 9090
  - Gympie Office - 5482 4177
  - Maroochydore Office - 5453 1888
- Elder Abuse Prevention Unit 1300 651 192
- Translating & Interpreting Service 131 450
- Suncoast Cooloola Outreach Prevention And Education 21

Useful Websites:

- Aboriginal & Torres Strait lsland Legal Service Ltd - www.atsils.com.au
- Australian Federal Police www.afp.gov.au
- Centrelink - www.centrelink.gov.au
- Caxton Legal Service - www.caxton.org.au
- Child Support Agency - www.justice.qld.gov.au
- Department of Immigration & Citizenship - www.immi.gov.au

- Department of Justice and Attorney General, QLD - www.justice.qld.gov.au
- DV Connect - www.dvconnect.org
- Elder Abuse Prevention Unit - www.eapu.com.au
- Family Court of Australia - www.familycourt.gov.au
- Immigrant Women's Support Service - www.iwss.org.au
- Legal Aid - www.legalaid.qld.gov.au
- Lifeline - www.lifeline.org.au
- National Missing Persons Unit - www.missingpersons.gov.au
- Office for Women - www.wis.sa.gov.au
- Office of Adult Guardian - www.justice.qld.gov.au/guardian/ag.htm
- Parentline - www.parentline.com.au
- QLD Aged & Disability Advocacy Inc. - www.qada.org.au
- QLD Association of Independent Legal Services Inc. - www.qails.org.au

QLD Department of Communities:

- Violence Prevention - www.communities.qld.gov.au/communityservices/violenceprevention
- Housing & Homelessness Service - www.communities.qld.gov.au/housing/housing-and-homelessnessservices
- QLD Department of Housing - www.qld.gov.au/housing
- QLD Police Service - www.police.qld.gov.au
- QLD Law Society - www.qls.com.au
- Sexual Assault Helpline - www.istaysafe.com/sexualassault
- Sunshine Coast Legal Service Inc. - www.suncoastcommunitylegal.org
- Sunshine Coast Regional Council - www.sunshinecoast.qld.gov.au
- Welfare Rights - www.wrcqld.org.au
- Women's Legal Service - www.wlsq.org.au
- Women with Disabilities Australia - www.wwda.org.au
- White Ribbon - www.whiteribbon.org.au

New Zealand:

- Domestic Violence Crisis Line - https://womensrefuge.org.nz/

United States:

- National Domestic Violence Hotline - https://www.thehotline.org/
- Resources for victims and survivors of domestic violence national crisis organizations and assistance - https://ncadv.org/resources

United Kingdom:

- National Domestic Abuse Helpline - https://www.nationaldahelpline.org.uk/

South Africa:

- Tears – bringing hope and healing - https://www.tears.co.za/

China:

- Maple - http://www.maple.org.cn/

Canada:

- Victim Link BC - https://www2.gov.bc.ca/gov/content/justice/criminal-justice/victims-of-crime/victimlinkbc

BIBLIOGRAPHY

Source: Cycle of violence:
http://www.dvhelppenrithregion.nsw.gov.au/index.php?option=com_content HYPERLINK

*Domestic Violence statistics from govt website:
https://www.aihw.gov.au/reports-data/behaviours-risk-factors/domestic-violence/overview

Lilly, M & Valdez, C 2012. 'Interpersonal Trauma and PTSD: The Roles of Gender and a Lifespan Perspective in Predicting Risk', *Psychological Trauma: Theory, Research, Practice, and Policy*, no. 4, pp. 140-144.

http://www.ncdsv.org/images/PowerControlwheelNOSHADING.pdf

O'Rourke, J, Tallman, B & Altmaier, E 2008, 'Measuring Post-Traumatic Changes in Spirituality/Religiosity'. *Mental Health, Religion, & Culture*, vol. 11, pp. 719-728.

Ozbay, F, Johnson, D, Dimoulas, E, Morgan, C, Charney, D & Southwick, S 2007, 'Social Support and Resilience to Stress: From Neurobiology to Clinical Practice'. *Psychiatry*, May, pp. 35-40.

Slavin-Spenny, O, Cohen, J, Oberleitner, L & Lumley, M 2010, 'The Effects of Different Methods of Emotional Disclosure: Differentiating Post-Traumatic Growth from Stress Symptoms'. *Journal of Clinical Psychology*, vol. 67, pp. 993-1007.

Other References

Berger, R & Weiss, T 2006, 'Posttraumatic Growth in Latina Immigrants' *Journal of Immigrant and Refugee Studies*, vol. 4, pp. 55-72.

Berger, R & Weiss, T 2008, 'The Posttraumatic Growth Model: An Expansion to the Family System', *Traumatology*, Nov, pp. 63–74

Carr, BI & Steel, J (ed.) 2013, *Psychological aspects of cancer a guide to emotion and psychological consequences of cancer, their causes and their management.* Springer, New York.

Costa, PT & McCrae, RR 1992, 'Normal Personality Assessment In Clinical Practice: The NEW Personality Inventory'. *Psychological Assessment*, vol. 4, pp. 5-13.

Flynn-Burhoe, M 2008, Abdu'l-Bahá on Suffering and Tests, Baha'i International Community, accessed Jul 14 2013, https://hdcommittee.wordpress.com/

Iversen, TN, Christiansen, DM, & Elklit, A 2011, 'Forskellige prædiktorer for posttraumatisk vækst på mikro-, meso-, og makroniveau'. *Psyke & Logos*, 32. vol. 2, pp. 321–348

Linley, PA & Joseph, S 2004, 'Positive Change Following Trauma and Adversity: A Review'. *Journal of Traumatic Stress*, vol. 17, pp. 11–21.

McAdams, DP 1993, *The Stories We Live By: Personal Myths and the Making of the Self*. New York: Morrow.

Neimeyer, RA 2001, *Meaning Reconstruction and the Experience of Loss*. American Psychological Association, Washington, DC.

Schoulte, J, Sussman, Z, Tallman, B, Munni, D, Cormick, C & Altier, E 2012, 'Is There Growth in Grief: Measuring Posttraumatic Growth in the Grief Response'. *Open Journal of Medical Psychology*, vol. 1, no. 3, pp. 38-43

Tedeschi, RG & Calhoun, LG 1995, *Trauma and Transformation: Growing in the Aftermath of Suffering.* Sage Publications, Thousand Oaks, California.

Tedeshi, RG & Calhoun, LG 1996, 'The Posttraumatic Growth Inventory: Measuring the Positive Legacy of Trauma'. *Journal of Traumatic Stress*, vol. 9, pp. 455-471.

Tedeshi, RG & Calhoun, LG 2004, *Posttraumatic Growth: Conceptual Foundation and Empirical Evidence.* Lawrence Erlbaum Associates, Philadelphia, Pennsylvania.

Tracey Angel Psychology

BIOGRAPHY

Kristina is a successful business owner, based on the Sunshine Coast. Kristina's main passions in life are her love of family, food and wine. Kristina's purpose in life is to empower as many people as possible to reach their full potential. Her personal mission statement is:

"Be positive always, enrich others with the spirit of optimism and hope through self-belief".

CONTACT US

Find us on Facebook:

The Self-Preservation Guide

www.ingramcontent.com/pod-product-compliance
Lightning Source LLC
Chambersburg PA
CBHW062021290426
44108CB00024B/2737